The Problem of the Negro as
a Problem for Gender

Forerunners: Ideas First

Short books of thought-in-process scholarship, where intense analysis, questioning, and speculation take the lead

FROM THE UNIVERSITY OF MINNESOTA PRESS

(Continued on page 82)

The Problem of the Negro as a Problem for Gender

Marquis Bey

University of Minnesota Press

MINNEAPOLIS

LONDON

ISBN 978-1-5179-1195-9 (PB)
ISBN 978-1-4529-6582-6 (Ebook)
ISBN 978-1-4529-6611-3 (Manifold)

Published by the University of Minnesota Press, 2020
111 Third Avenue South, Suite 290
Minneapolis, MN 55401-2520
http://www.upress.umn.edu

Available as a Manifold edition at manifold.umn.edu

The University of Minnesota is an equal-opportunity educator and employer.

Contents

Preface

I BEGIN with a brooding frustration. A problem, if you will. That frustration, that problem, however, yielded all of this. So, while frustrating, the problem was necessary; it gifted me, us, with all that lies before you, all of these thoughts—indeed, as a problem, it gifted me, us, as such, *thought*. While frustrating, the problem precipitated the emergence of the very thing that demonstrates the utility, the generativity, of problems.

I have only been calling myself a scholar of black studies and transgender studies for five years at the time of this writing. In that time, I have come across, on occasion after occasion, the illustrious name of Nahum Chandler. Whenever reference to black thought arose, or the figure of the Negro, or "paraontology," Chandler's name followed almost immediately, a citational nod that couldn't not be made. But that was often what it was—a nod, a quick slip of the conceptual, philosophical brand name, as it were, perhaps a brief subsequent foray into a quoted or paraphrased definition, and then back to originally scheduled academic programming. I wanted to know more. Who was this Chandler guy, this powerhouse who seemed to loom large yet whose words, whose deep cogitative archive, often went ungrappled with? So, I set out to read his opus: *X—the Problem of the Negro as a Problem for Thought*.

I'm not going to say that that was a mistake, but I will say, with an unwavering fortification, that it was a stupid idea at the time.

Reading Chandler's work made very clear why he was only referenced rather than deeply, sustainedly engaged, why he was known mostly through the buzzwords and not the archive on which the buzzwords rested. The man is difficult to read; reading X is a treacherous discursive experience. One cannot leisurely read Chandler; one must strap in, come correct, bring one's A+ game, and, in the immortal words of *The Lion King*'s Scar, *be prepared*. I was not prepared my first time reading it. I could not commit, could not get past "Anacrusis." So I gave it up for months, contenting myself with the secondary literature and references to that behemoth of a text. That is, until the resounding pulsations of the "X," its polysemous and promiscuous applications, compelled me to return.

This book, what you hold in your hands—more of a pamphlet actually, a speculative wandering around the circulatory system of a problematic and problematizing thought—culminated because of my frustration with the difficulty of Chandler's writing yet the perceived (and, in my opinion, confirmed) importance of a deep engagement with it, the love of thinkers who oft made references to Chandler (Fred Moten, J. Kameron Carter, Denise Ferreira da Silva), and lastly, the thing that made me dive deep into the Chandlerian thickets, his profound oversights as to the massive resonances the X-as-Negro problematic and problematic figure of the Negro have with the X as referential of the gender nonnormative, the trans.

What I have written here is thus an attempt to take Chandler's book, and his overall intellectual corpus, to task on its radical reconfiguration of "the figure of the Negro" as a disturbance of ontological groundedness and, more pressingly, its elision of the gendered valences of such ontological disturbance. Insofar as Chandler's work is deeply generative in theorizing the figure of the Negro as both a "historial" figure and a nonfigure, as it were, that undoes the ontological moorings that sustain the violent logics of metaphysics, *The Problem of the Negro as a Problem for Gender* pushes this in a more radical direction by amplifying the figural nature (or the not-quite-material nature) of "the Negro" and excavating the deeply gendered, *trans* resonances not considered in Chandler's incredible book. This book, then, seeks to contribute two primary things. First is a deep reading and writing-with Chandler's theorization of the X and the Negro. Part of the lack of sustained engagement with the full scope of Chandler's work is his esoteric writing, which I hope to clarify. Not only do I hope to elucidate Chandler's theorizations but I also hope to excavate the gendered elisions in theorizations of the Negro as an ontological problem. That is, I am bringing the trans and transgender studies to bear on the methodological critique of the ontology of whiteness so pervasive now in black studies. Therefore, second, I contribute an argument in excess of, though conversant with, Chandler in that I draw readers into a meditation on black feminism and gender nonnormativity via the X. *The Problem of the Negro as a Problem for Gender* is interested in how gender, specifically trans genders, nonbinary genders, and the nonnormative gender implied by the nexus of black and woman, are necessary for any radical project of interrogating the logics of Western ontology.

Problem?

> ... making no effort to do away with this problem once
> and for all.
>
> —GILLES DELEUZE AND FÉLIX GUATTARI, *Anti-Oedipus:*
> *Capitalism and Schizophrenia*

FOR YEARS, perhaps since my youth, I have been intrigued by
problems. In a world in which so many seek solutions to all the
troubling, fussy problems out there, I was one who enjoyed the
problems themselves, those units of vexing ebullience. And the
more they eluded solutions, the better. Problems to me were
much more interesting because they cause a bit of a ruckus,
get people all riled up and ready to do something about them.
Solutions, on the other hand, stopped everything. It was always
the problems that got things going. The intriguing part was the
problematizing, as problems became problems because they
did something: they problematized. And the problematizing, I
examined, allowed for the jostling of the very things I believed
to be worthy of being jostled.

That felicitous noun has a rich etymology, a strand of which
is defined in alignment with its more common definition as "a
matter or situation regarded as unwelcome, harmful, or wrong
and needing to be overcome." This marks problems as imped-
iments to be surmounted. Problems serve no positive purpose,
only a negative roadblock to progress. It is no surprise, then,
that problems have caught a bad rap. But examining a different

etymological trajectory in asymptotic relation to the former, we discover that a problem can more succinctly be described as "a difficult or demanding question." Problems are no mere things in themselves that, transparently, have meanings or effects in need of overcoming. They express a certain agency and, indeed, demand a reckoning. And yet in the vociferous demand, it is nevertheless never entirely, or even marginally, certain what that demand is. Thus, the demand, while still present, straddles a teetering chasm met as a radical indeterminacy, an unmitigated uncertainty.

Because I also grew up around people who have a history of utter coolness, that *black cool* known as an *"intelligence of the soul"* that "stirs the imagination," "problem" was never permitted to remain in its lexical strictures dictated by standard English.[1] It gained a lilting flutter that made it something slightly different. Problems could not be mere things to be solved, especially from a problem people, as it were ("How does it feel to be a problem?" Du Bois intonates, ventriloquizing his white interlocutors); problems had to actualize themselves in different ways. So they took on the meaning of something not quite discernible. Imagine: someone looks at you askance, too skewed to be read as innocuous, so you ask, "Problem?" Or, you are listening to a throwback track, Lil Scrappy's and Trillville's "No Problem," and hear, over that melodiously eerie instrumental and stipples of "Okay-kay-kaaay," "But you don't want no problem (problem, hoo!)." Or further, you realize that time and again its pronunciation is much closer to "prollum," a vernacular rejoinder to coercions of "proper" diction. Problems signify here something like a generative waver. In the interrogative form, it portends an unsettling of norms of courteous interaction. In the musical

1. Rebecca Walker, *Black Cool: One Thousand Streams of Blackness* (Berkeley, Calif.: Soft Skull Press, 2012), 64, 80.

sense, it acts as an enticing threat, something attractive for its mystery but, too, frightening because of it. And as a vernacular tinkering, one knows but initially cannot be sure of the word one is hearing, its pronunciation obscuring something as it illuminates another way to encounter the very thing being obscured.

It strikes me that problems in these senses orbit around an understanding of the term as indicative of an indeterminate obscuration. Or alternatively, problems—somewhere between connoting and denoting—*ghost* meaning, leaving the encounter with them in a state of specific unspecificity. A problem thus presents a charged space of indeterminacy. Such indeterminacy generates the possibility of something profound happening at the level of the micropolitical, the molecular, wherein small tinkerings yield micro-abrasions that dissolve the sedimented regimes structuring our horizons. In alignment with my paraontological obsessions—that is, the radical effects of blackness and gender nonnormativity or transness—problems index, in their tinkering, molecular and molar, the animative "black operations that will produce the absolute overturning, the absolute turning of this motherfucker out."[2] It is because of the utility of problems, their expressivity of something to be learned via their opening up of normative seams, that I wish to dwell on them, that I have dwelled on them since my youth, and now in my maturity through, again, my obsessions of blackness and gender nonnormativity.

Illuminative of my opening epigraph is the simple fact that problems are not problematic. Indeed, they problematize and open space for inquiry, inserting a richness via rupture in the smoothness of decorum, but they are not problematic in the negative sense of stalling progress or being unjust. Only if we

2. Fred Moten, "Blackness and Nothingness (Mysticism in the Flesh)," *South Atlantic Quarterly* 112, no. 4 (2013): 742.

mean the puncturing of the violence of the unexamined quotidian can we say problems are problematic; only if we mean
to honor the pricking characteristic of the *punctum* jamming
the machinic *studium,* as the *punctum*'s mere presence shifts
the interpretive gaze, permitted a renewed encounter via its
snapping of the quotidian, the metaphysical, the ontological,
Barthes has said.[3] While Deleuze and Guattari are referencing,
in the epigraph, the impediment of psychoanalysis's bourgeois
repression to liberation, I excerpt them here to suggest that problems need not be solved at all; indeed, problems ought not be
solved, as it is the problematizing function that generates what
Deleuze and Guattari are calling "genuine liberation." The onset
of problems' problematizing engenders that milieu of uncertainty and indeterminacy, which, by virtue of its fracturing—or
its "fractual," to use the language of my key interlocutor in this
text, Nahum Chandler—presents the possibility of exploring the
ghosts in the machine, as it were, precisely because of its own
ghosting of a meaning that abides the machinic logics mooring
normativity in place.

Problem and its lexical derivatives (problematic, problematize, problematization) proliferate through Chandler's text, and
rightly so, as the term is precisely the organizing concept (or
perhaps I should say, with Chandler's preferences in mind, a
concept-metaphor or, even better, paraconcept) for the figure of
the Negro. Certainly, he gains *problem*'s efficacy from Du Bois's
quite famous opening scene in which many a white person skirts
around the question "How does it feel to be a problem?" to which
Du Bois responds, "Seldom a word." But what is being done with
problem and its derivatives is the work of ontological critique.
Before addressing Chandler, I might offer a reading of Du Bois

3. Roland Barthes, *Camera Lucida: Reflections on Photography,*
trans. Richard Howard (New York: Hill and Wang, 1981), 42.

first, as "How does it feel to be a problem"—which is for him, he says, *the real question*—is an ontological query: it is in effect a question of what it means to *be* a, the, problem, affectively. To answer "seldom a word" is a nonresponse that registers at the level of Being inasmuch as the seldom word answered by the being that is a problem for Being problematizes Being as such. Put differently, a reading of Du Bois that converses with Chandler's, that is perhaps the second verse of the track Chandler is putting down, is one in which Du Bois's nonresponse is the problematizing of his problematic status precisely because his problematic status is the result of the philosophical project of ontology that he, in his concerted beingness as a nonresponse, cannot not critique.

Chandler accentuates this via his elaboration on the impossibility of asking the question of Being, which is to say the impossibility of encountering Being on innocent grounds. From the jump, ontology is fraught and given to obscuring its intentions. To ask the question of Being is to inhabit its fraughtness that, in an inhabitation of it, disallows one to ask it the question of itself that must be asked. Asking of it the question that must be asked yields the conclusion, Chandler says, that "*the question* destroys itself" (3; emphasis original). It is in this destruction that another terrain or logic—"an other logic, logic *of* the other" (5; emphasis original) of which we are in the midst—can be unleashed to luminous effect. Or, darkened effects.

These effects fall under various headings in Chandler's text, one of which is instructive here: the heading of "Africanist problematics" (15). To be sure, as will be made clear, lovingly and hopefully humbly, throughout this meditation, my concerns exceed the paradoxically capacious parochialism of Chandler's readings. That is, Chandler's illustrious reading misses certain opportunities to think rigorously about the "paraconcept" of gender or, more specifically, transness/gender nonnormativity, as well as the utility of his conception of the X as a figurative to highlight gendered valences. Still instructive here is the potently racial notion of Africanist problematics in that it should be understood as the problematizing engendered by blackness (a term Chandler actually rarely uses, preferring other terms, such as the *Negro* or *African American*). It, or they, Africanist problematics, articulate groundedness's problem; they are problems for grounds and groundedness, or first principles, origins and primordial purities. Chandler's itinerary by way of Du Bois's is one that follows around a certain rift, a rending of the philosophical mainstay of essence, or a first principle, of a ground, and finally of pure being, all of which are troubled by the problematization of the figure of the Negro, the African American, the "X." The move I wish to make here is that the Africanist problematic, insofar as it raises the *general* question—a generality that proliferates throughout *X—the Problem of the Negro as a Problem for Thought* and that I find conceptually compelling as it gets us outside of specificities that often disallow capacious and coalitional thinking—of "the possibility and ground of being" (52), is one that rigorously excavates the possibility of another kind of subjective generality. The raising of the general question of Being requires us to vitiate all that such a question has ushered forth, which is, of course, everything. That this also dissolves all borders concerning the "human," including, Chandler says, "gender," I am drawn to the operative role of, as it were, gender problematics.

Let us inscribe this a bit differently. The Negro's questioning and problematizing of the ground of pure being gets us to question then the human and necessarily the things that constitute the human, including the animal and sexual difference and gender—and perhaps beyond this. Though others might be itching to say that gender is *more* and *originarily* constitutive of the human, to say that gender comes before the Negro viz. race, I am uninterested in making such a move. I will say, however, that the Negro, while not at all a comfortable inhabitant of gender as such, is differentiated along lines of what *might be* called gender. By this I do not mean simply that black "women" are "multiply marginalized" but something more incisive: that the figure of the Negro, that blackness, animates and instrumentalizes gender always toward its dissolution. The Negro and its figurative problematization is presumed by Chandler as, ironically, "purely" "under the heading of" race without accounting for how this is at once a general problematic and thus a problem for gender as well as problematized *through* gender. It is not so much that I disagree with Chandler than that I want to critique and radicalize him on the behalf of his own thought. The gesture of problematization is a good and necessary one that must reckon with the ontological problematic of gender through and *for* the Negro, which is then to say through and for the nonsubstitutable vectors that compose ontology as such.

The forms this meditation on problematizing will take are, in Chandler's preferential term, the Negro and, extending Chandler beyond his elisions, gender, or more specifically, the trans and gender nonnormative. The Negro problem, inflective and definitional of the vitiation of the typical, unhindered goings-on of sociality, dovetails lusciously with what might be understood as the gender problem, or the way the ghosted presence (which is to say, the way that the trans ghosts or evanesces corporealized meaning) of gender nonnormativity vitiates the founding attempts to make legible through a grounding in binary gender.

To advance these problems, the X serves as instructive. As the "X" carries with it historical valences that Chandler finds useful in terms of racial distinction (his preferred terminology over "race")[4]

4. "Racial distinction" connotes a way of acknowledging that what has come to be called race is a mechanism by which difference

and that I find useful in terms of designating trans or nonbinary genders, the letter threads this brief text and highlights blackness and gender nonnormativity by way of their expressivity through it. In short, X functions throughout as a link between the problematizing done by blackness and the problematizing done by gender nonnormativity, or transness. It becomes the critical site of articulating blackness and transness as expressive through each other that is not a reduction to conflation. X is the coalescing of these two problems, indexical of their tricky indeterminacy and besidedness to ontologization.

In clarification, X can act as a problematizing anagrammar that intensifies (not consolidates) the dissonance effectuated by the Negro and, differently yet relatedly, the trans. To return to the opening discussion of *problem*'s valences, if X has a history, as I'll show explicitly in the second half of this text, of alluding to the evanescing effects of the Negro and the trans, this convergence functions as a tray of indeterminacy and opening. To ask "Problem?" as a way to address, or rather unaddress, inasmuch as the query notes nothing but the laceration of meaning-as-assumed, a slight the condition of possibility for which is normality itself; or to hear Lil Scrappy's and Trillville's choral refrain as a paradoxically seductive danger, the mysteriousness of which is a *différance* in the dark; or to incite the vernacular pronunciation "prollum" as, allowing Gilles Deleuze and Henry Louis Gates Jr. to converse, a difference and repetition with a difference—where "prollum" is an anoriginal differentiation and dispersal tied to a

---

is mapped and, subsequently, made to subjectivate people through the inscriptions of the constructed differences. Whereas to simply say race, on Chandler's account, "reproduce[s] not only this concept, but thereby implicitly affirm[s] the violence of the practices carried out in its name," racial distinction sidesteps the violence by not presuming its naturalness and instead notes its political, instrumental underpinnings (49).

sociohistorical commentary via grammatical underminings—is all to suggest in different ways the desedimentary effects of the problems by the names of the Negro and the trans. "X" highlights and intensifies these effects.

In a sense, the terms *Negro* and *trans* can behave in this way because of their generalization rather than, as is typical, their specificity. By way of Chandler's pursuit to think the racialized "double consciousness" as not confined to the African American subject but indicative of how we all come into subjectivity, there is an ontological allowance with these terms. They stand in for a process that has been mapped onto certain subjectivities and has been inaccurately presumed to be categorically destined for, and bounded by, those subjectivities. But the delinking expands the processes through the terms, terms that reference what Chandler remarks as "the historical form of the problematization of existence" (12). The historical, or perhaps I should more accurately say the historicized, embodied figures (which is to say conceptual apparatuses that have been made to live on corporealized subjects before and after interpellation) of the Negro and the transgender person may be the historical forms but are not the totality, nor the origins, of the black and the trans, I submit. They are the names that have been given to, and the kinds of bodies that have been made to live through, the problematization of existence.

Mere existence is disallowed an uncritiqued dwelling place in the world. Perturbing that existence, which is a modality of life that "overrepresents" itself as life-as-such through colonial imposition, the Negro (blackness intensified) and the trans (gender nonnormativity intensified) do the work of "unsettling."[5]

5. See Sylvia Wynter, "Unsettling the Coloniality of Being/ Power/Truth/Freedom: Towards the Human, after Man, Its Overrepresentation—an Argument," *CR: The New Centennial Review* 3, no. 3 (2004): 257–337, https://doi.org/10.1353/ncr.2004.0015.

Finely put, if I may signpost in brutal clarity what I will be up to, this brief book takes Chandler's Du Boisian argument in *X—the Problem of the Negro as a Problem for Thought* as not merely a meditation on blackness by way of an examination of Du Bois's oeuvre but also apt for a meditation, here, on problematic genders. That is, through the paraontological, the between, and the figure of the X (with its explicit contemporary link to nonbinary and trans genders as showcased, for example, in neologisms like "Latin*x*"), there is a generative co-reading to be done between the Negro's problematizing and trans's problematizing. Chandler's text serves as both an argumentative tool for rendering the "radical alternative" in and as blackness as well as demonstrating, if only in its interstitial folds where my readings might nuzzle closely to mis- or overreadings, the necessarily gendered valences of that radical alternative. The Negro indexes processes of racialization in which race is a materialization of hegemony's disciplining of unruliness and irregularity. The Negro—indexical of blackness—serves as the corporeal consolidation of such a primordial irregularity. It bears being noted, then, that the question of gender always rests alongside the question of race, or more pointedly, formations of gender are always iterations of race; gender serves often as a racial (re)arrangement.[6] Insofar as the problematization of gender finds expression in the trans, and insofar as gender constitutes the scope of ontology and the grounds of being, it must also be said that the problem of the Negro is, via its concatenation with transness, a problem for gender.

6. See C. Riley Snorton, *Black on Both Sides: A Racial History of Trans Identity* (Minneapolis: University of Minnesota Press, 2017); see also Jules Gill-Peterson, *Histories of the Transgender Child* (Minneapolis: University of Minnesota Press, 2018).

Paraontology

> . . . the challenge of calling an object into being without
> owning or being owned by the call of identity or identifica-
> tion, of recognition or acknowledgment.
>
> —STEPHEN BEST, *None Like Us: Blackness, Belonging,*
> *Aesthetic Life*

THE *PARAONTOLOGICAL DISTINCTION*. That is Chandler's
task in so many ways, to clarify and flesh out this distinction. It
proceeds by way of a general critical practice, a general desedimentation concerned with the mode or dimension or order—
whatever metaphor of your choosing—of this distinction, that
is, the conception of difference among humans and nonhumans
and other-than-humans understood through the concepts,
chiefly, of race and gender. (Chandler, though, would drop the
qualifiers and thereafter simply notate the distinction as "difference among humans understood as . . .") It is a distinction that
unmoors the ligaments of ontology, inclusive of identities held
dearly like those of race and gender, in the service of what J.
Kameron Carter and Sarah Jane Cervenak refer to as "paraontological life."[1] I am understanding the paraontological project

1. Sarah Jane Cervenak and J. Kameron Carter, "Untitled and
Outdoors: Thinking with Saidiya Hartman," *Women and Performance: A
Journal of Feminist Theory* 27, no. 1 (2017): 53–54n3, https://doi.org/10.1
080/0740770X.2017.1282116. They describe paraontological life as "the

as a stringent, radical attempt to explore other modes of living. These modes of living might cause the death of a subject, but that is only the death of a subject that needs to measure up to ontological grammars. Paraontological life, subjectivity emerging through paraontology, can look quite different, and it is that kind of life we strive toward. We get closer to it with the attenuation of each vector of ontological entrapment we manage to grittily, painstakingly abandon.

The concept of the paraontological cannot be "reduced" or "simplified" to any one thing, its elusiveness perhaps its primary point. It is, crucially, not really a concept to be pointed to; more closely to truth, paraontology concerns the effective loosening of concepts to which we can point. Indeed, it bears a certain relation to Derrida's *différance*, a term famously deemed a "non-concept" to refer to the difference and deferral of meaning. Pertinently, *différance* has been described by Derrida—after much frustration with an audience member who likened the term to the god of negative theology—as precisely the unknowable source of everything, and precisely not that at all. Attentive listeners can hear the reverberatory echoes of an Ellisonian, and later Marlon Riggsian, declaration: "I said black is . . . an' black ain't . . . ," and also pertinently, "Black will make you . . . or black will un-make you."[2]

A few clarification points, via Chandler: paraontology names "the project of a desedimentation; it is genealogical and deconstructive, yet neither; a desedimentation of the status of the distinctions among beings, a critical account of their ostensible ground or predication, and a critical reconsideration of the

---

undercommon otherside of paraontology, namely, a modality of life unmoored from ownership, (en)titlement, groundedness, and settlement."

2. Ralph Ellison, *Invisible Man* (New York: Random House, 2002); Marlon Riggs, dir., *Tongues Untied* (1989).

hierarchies and orientations by which they are articulated or understood as in relation." It also rejects an absolute mark or determination, rejects, that is, a categorical distinction, purity.[3] Desedimentation is taken, with some license, from Derrida, one of Chandler's primary interlocutors. He shares an anecdote, one, on his account, he had never shared in public before until his annotations on the Negro as a problem for thought during a Society for the Humanities lecture at Cornell University I attended in 2018. As is his wont, he spoke slowly, and swayed slowly yet, ironically, dizzyingly. His voice deep and commanding, again as is his wont. He shared that while in Chicago—the city of which I am now a denizen—he walked around the University of Chicago's campus discussing with Derrida desedimentation. Derrida at that point found desedimentation a more convincing notion than deconstruction as a metaphor system or network. Derrida gave, Chandler says, a proverbial "thumbs up." What Derrida wrote as "de-sedimentation" implies an undoing of the work of sedimentation, the consolidation that occurs in thought (a thought often given to forms of commodification). Chandler makes it his preferential term for its radical fundamentality, or potential for a radically fundamental loosening. And he links this with the movement of difference and differentiation, the proliferative unhinging effects of the movement of differentiation: "Such difference, or movement of difference, not only proposes the possibility of a desedimentation of the presumption of purity, or pure being, inhabited as a problem and problematic by Africanist thinkers, but it would also remark the most fundamental dimension of the configured possibility of that which could, perhaps, be considered new in the

3. Nahum D. Chandler, "Paraontology; or, Notes on the Practical Theoretical Politics of Thought" (2018), https://vimeo.com/297769615.

world in general and in any sense" (18). This is paraontology, the paraontologically distinctive movement.

This movement, to continue in the Derridean vein with a blackened twist, if you will—or ceding the nonexistent ground to what can only be a black and blackened Derrida—refuses to give definition or essence to purportedly extant historical figures precisely because, via the desedimentary, deconstructive, *différantial* workings of thinking these subjects, there is to be found no definition or last essential analysis. The deconstructive work of desedimentation, its paraontological sinews and ligaments, is, if you'll allow me this neologism, nondefinessential. Because of this, we cannot and can never distinguish between who or what is within or without the ostensible boundaries of the very thing we mark as possessing a transparent definition or essence. Hence, the criteria for inclusion and exclusion dissolve into nothingness, thus making the work of paraontology the recognition of this dissolution and, from there, joyfully conceding that there are no criteria for subjective verification, no ontological ground on which to stand in order to be viable, and indeed a no-groundedness that invites subjects into it as a place to stand, para- and non- and nega-ontologically. Paraontology, then, reading Derrida both into and out from this, characterizes an uncertainty principle: not merely an undecidability but an intentional impossibility to determine what is inside and outside the subjective, ontological threshold. So, there *is no* threshold. The door swings marvelously open for entry into the effects of blackness; there are no regulatory criteria for those who might take up the impure and desedimentary effects of the figure of the Negro, those deployed Africanist rumblings. In this is the radical "suggestion of the possibility of a general desedimentation of a traditional conceptual premise that organizes the interpretation of the African American subject in the United States," a premise fixated on bestowals of sufficient measurements of ancestry or blood quantum or byzantine criteria for authenticity as definitive for one's status as black. Doing this, Chandler concludes, "assist[s] further in opening a new way of thinking the question of the African American or African diasporic subject, the implications of which might bear force on our understanding of the modes of constitution of any historical subject"—this new way being one that has wrecked the purity of ontological grounding so much as to dislodge the aforementioned organizing premises as regulatory qualifications for the problematics indexical in the Negro, making the figure of the Negro, blackness, and Africanist thinking possible for constituting *any* subject who bears a desedimentary relationship to ontological mandates, for the Negro, blackness, and Africanist thinking name that impurifying process, somatically indiscriminately so (135). So, again, there is no—or a refusal of, a displacement and exorbitance of—ontology and the purity upon which the figure of the Negro, in its paraontology, rests. And that is nothing short of salvific.

The ontological predicate of purity signifies strongly in terms of gender too, with there being a long history of (white) women being subject to and deploying notions of purity. At times, white feminist women garnered a sense of moral capital on the concept of "purity," specifically sexual purity, which then acted as the legitimizing force for their valid claim to womanhood and, through this, respect and dignity believed to have been denied them. At other times, white feminism (an albeit nebulous term too often assumed to be readily intelligible), and some other types of feminisms, mobilized a sense of gendered essentialism or pure category of "woman" that needed to be restored, recovered, and wielded to shore up women's rights claims.[4] Purity, then, on the ontological level, is significantly gendered, and the

4. See Susan Stryker, *Transgender History: The Roots of Today's Revolution* (Berkeley, Calif.: Seal Press, 2017), 125.

ontological grounds vitiated by paraontology's desedimentation is a markedly ungendered move as well, a trans move.

The site of the movement is placed under the heading (a phrase I adopt from Chandler's consistent use) of originarity. Originarity is not to be reduced to, or understood as, an origin with all its attending purity. The contrary is at work here. It is deployed as a "scene of possibility" (17), which I read as in convivial harmony with an understanding of transitivity, where the latter is a (trans)gender inflected primordially proliferative scene. Originarity as a scene of exorbitant (chapter 1) possibility spills into transitivity as a sort of Pangaea where the trans thinks across registers of species and, moreover, indexes the incohering of gender, sex, and anatomical indices of gender.[5] Through both these registers, desedimentation takes place; originarity and transitivity precipitate desedimentation, giving over anything that might be considered new, like different formations of subjectivity. (Its texture is consolidated succinctly at the outset of X in Chandler's description of the Los Angeles rebellion that took place in the year of my birth: as "an explosion, an irruption somewhere, from the beginning of time, as time, and thus yet beyond time, neither time nor not time, indeed displacing time, before beginning, cavernous and massive, fractual, infinitely so" [2].)

These new formations arise through paraontology, for to arise via ontology would be to be already enthralled in the philosophical mandates regulating what can ontologically appear, what can be captured by ontology. The paraontological is how the Negro emerges or the trans emerges, both of which

5. See Snorton in C. Riley Snorton and T Fleischmann, "C. Riley Snorton and T Fleischmann Talk Gender, Freedom, and Transitivity," interviewed by V. V. Ganeshananthan and Whitney Terrell, March 7, 2019, https://lithub.com/c-riley-snorton-and-t-fleischmann-talk-gender-freedom-and-transitivity/.

find expression—as will be discussed in detail in subsequent chapters—in the figure of the X.

In short, forwarded in Chandler is a notion of a paraontology that functions as a critical concept that breaks up and desediments. By way of this, it permits the rewriting of narratives and the very conditions of understanding the present as such. Importantly, the goal is not to create a different, alternative ontology. Paraontology is not a search for new categories, as if categorization is a neutral process. It is not; categorization is a mechanism of ontology, an apparatus of circumscription. What the paraontological suggests is a dissolution. As a project of desedimentation, it takes categorizations, namely, "race" for Chandler but extensive in its identificatory assaults, which then includes a category such as gender, and wishes to "make tremble" any kind of "sedimented commitments" that maintain in place (5). This making tremble staunchly refuses to permit subjective lodgings into place, those processes that end the possibility of mutability. Being and becoming other than we must, or other than we are said to be able to by ontological mandates, is to find life and livability in mutability and rearrangement toward the illegible, which is to say the defiance of the ontological—in other words, the paraontological. Subjective and existential trembling, "ontological" trembling, is the reconfigurative life for which we search; it is paraontological life.

Interestingly, the prefixal *para-* comes from the Greek word *παρα-*, meaning "by the side of," "beside," and hence "alongside, by, past, or beyond." It also bears the sense of cognate adverbial prepositions like "to one side, aside, amiss, faulty, *irregular, disordered, improper,* wrong." Additionally, however, as a second prefixal etymology, *para-* is linked to French, Italian, and classical Latin words for to make ready, prepare, defend from, or shelter; it is affixed to words with the sense of "protection from ____." Often when *para-* has been invoked in philosophical theorizations, it has only been used in the first sense, which importantly bears a strong etymological affinity with *trans* (to the side of, across, beyond). I wish to explore the implications of thinking the *para-* of *paraontology* in both etymological senses, denoting the paraontologicality of blackness and transness as a fissuring besidedness to ontic and ontological meaning making *and* a protection from the regime of ontology, which is to say, defended from the tyrannies of hegemonic, stabilizing subjectivation. (Because, after all, despite my own critical position relative to his work, Calvin Warren's assessment of ontology as the field in which blackness is cursed by Being as unintelligible and "execrated" from it is apt.)[6] Hence, not only are blackness and transness beside ontology as its insidious simmering sibling but it is sheltered from the normalizing forces of that ontology, definitionally refusitive of being affected by that ontology. They are moves of refusing ontology *as a form of* emerging otherwise, which is to say—that is, those forms that are otherwise emergences are to say—the Negro and the trans are problematizations of one another and the ontologically imposed claims that are race and gender. This is a profound site, in fact. Indeed, we learn about worlds when they do not accommodate us, and that refusal to accommodate is the marker of paraontology.[7] And problems, the Negro and trans, do not accommodate the worlds of race and gender.

In a simplistic sense, paraontology refers to something that

6. See specifically the chapter titled "The Question of Black Being," in Calvin L. Warren, *Ontological Terror: Blackness, Nihilism, and Emancipation,* 26–61 (Durham, N.C.: Duke University Press, 2018).

7. I am drawing here from Sara Ahmed and would be remiss if I did not quote the opening lines from her essay "Affinity of Hammers": "We learn about worlds when they do not accommodate us. Not being accommodated can be pedagogy. We generate ideas through the struggles we have to be in the world; we come to question worlds when we are in question." *TSQ* 3, no 1–2 (2016): 22.

cannot really be "referred" to. References hold sway by virtue of their allusions to something concrete, something rooted and grounded. A kind of sediment, if you will. Yet we know that, per Chandler, paraontology cannot refer to something in this way because paraontology is a project of desedimentation. I propose, then, the language of pulsation or resonance. Hence paraontology in a brief sense resonates with a meaning of that "which is yet to be thought," as Giorgio Agamben has offered.[8] I, and I submit Chandler, too, depart slightly from this understanding, inasmuch as Agamben says that paraontology is "an *ontology* which is yet to be thought." But I maintain here through my reading of Chandler that paraontology cannot be said to be another type of ontology; it is not ontology with a different, less normative name. More closely, the pulsation of paraontology exudes a meaning that appears as a "potential ontological alterity," where the alterity is one that contrasts with, or, more accurately, deviates from and destabilizes the point of reference for, ontology.[9] What arises nebulously, unintelligibly, in the interstices or beyond the scope of what can be understood has the residue of the paraontological. It is because to bring something into a certain legibility is to place it within the dictates of ontological constraints, to subject it to onto-epistemic templates that paraontology, by definition, eludes by way of a double gesture of being hailed by language but inadequately, hailed by insufficient language and thus only partially understood, which is in fact its wont.

There is theoretical work being done by paraontology. It is theoretical work that Chandler wants to think as critical theoretical

8. Delivered in a lecture titled "What Is a Paradigm?" at the European Graduate School on January 10, 2002.

9. Benjamin Alberti and Yvonne Marshall, "Animating Archaeology: Local Theories and Conceptually Open-Ended Methodologies," *Cambridge Archaeological Journal* 19, no. 3 (2009): 354, https://doi.org/10.1017/S0959774309000535.

fiction.[10] For critical theoretical fiction is not presumptive about its theoretical import as bearing a "real" or ontological relation to that which it theorizes, and this relinquishing of an ontological hold permits other moves to be made. This theoretical work, this paraontological work, goes under these names but cannot, in the final instance, go under any given name. The practice of naming emerges by way of the historial, as Chandler calls it, a staking of identification in the American ontological project, construed convincingly to the Western philosophical project of racial distinction and, I add, the gender binary and "coloniality of gender."[11] Paraontological theorizations and paraontology itself must be beyond any name as it is otherwise than a thought, properly understood. Thought in the philosophical tradition is oriented toward existence as being, which the Negro, the X, and, in my iteration, the trans all seek to undermine as they are projects of impurity and nonexistence. The name for the concern with impurity, with grounded irreverence, or irreverence for the ground, is paraontology.

So when meditating on the relationship between the Negro and the trans—or more specifically, blackness and transness, those indexical referents of corporeal transgression via a primordial mutiny—what arises is an entrée into a generative disruption.

10. He gets this from Spivak, who in an interview argues that Derrida theorizes deconstruction by way of a unifying theoretical fiction, a methodological presupposition that allows the work of deconstruction to begin in the middle, as it were. Theoretical fiction is the formulation for what must be posited but known to be not quite true in order for the work of deconstruction, or desedimentation, to proceed. See Gayatri Chakravorty Spivak, *The Post-colonial Critic: Interviews, Strategies, Dialogues* (New York: Psychology Press, 1990), 136.

11. See María Lugones, "The Coloniality of Gender," in *The Palgrave Handbook of Gender and Development: Critical Engagements in Feminist Theory and Practice*, ed. Wendy Harcourt, 13–33 (London: Palgrave Macmillan, 2016).

While history has consolidated these names into ontological facts that seem deeply particular and specific, it is nevertheless contingent upon the vagaries of history; history, in other words, as it has come to give heft to an understanding of blackness and transness as particular existential modes of living specific to those given (in and as) black and/or trans(gender) people, might be very viscerally felt as exclusive of those who do not measure up to preconceived somatic endowments of race and gender. It is not, however, the understanding displayed on the occasion of this meditation. It has been argued, persuasively, elsewhere by scholars like Claire Colebrook, C. Riley Snorton, Denise Ferreira da Silva, and Fred Moten that the black and trans of the ante- and antimatter are less measurements of the body—a body, we must note, that is not always epistemically certain of its nature and its effects—and instead, more substantively, denote a kind of anteoriginal displacement of sedimentation, a noncategorical movement away from definitive loci of corporeal and ontological knowledge. The thrust of this book, then, will operate under this mantle of blackness and transness as *trans*gressional: as what will become more evident as problematizing analytics.

Consider here the paraontological "movement of black thought":

> the internal production of racial ontologies of blackness by black diasporans have destabilized the claim that any racial category is given, or natural. Nahum Chandler has written of this double character of blackness as a fundamental problematic to any no-tion of categorisation because of its "paraontological" status. By this he means that any iteration of blackness involves the shat-tering of the basis of racial purity in all its forms, in the service of the affirmation of dehiscient non-exclusionary improvisations of collective being. The "paraontology" of blackness is the constant escape of blackness from the fixity of racial ontology that struc-tures white supremacy.[12]

12. Black Study Group, "The Movement of Black Thought—

Upon these logics Chandler calls the Negro a "paraconcept," and I might also call the trans a paraconcept—they are referents to desedimentary impurities that do the work of dislodging, respectively, racial and gender distinction, rather than figures that exist as such. To say that the Negro, or the trans, is an actually occurring self-evident entity in the world concedes to the very logics that someone like Du Bois is trying to oppose. That is, to concede uncritically that there is something called the Negro and that it exists, that it is obviously called and known as the Negro, is to affirm the logics behind the entity of the Negro, which brings with it also the violently racist formulations of it that would adhere to those hailed by that nominative. On the other hand, to say that the Negro, and the trans, are merely concepts is to bereft them of any kind of essence; to deem it a concept would, in a way, be a radically anti- or nonessentialist move. Theoretically and philosophically, such an argument might be fine, but *politically*— in an environ wherein something called the Negro and some people called transgender are deeply felt to exist and, on the grounds of that existence, are pulverized in so many ways—it is quite dangerous. In other words, the Negro cannot exist, but the Negro must exist. Black is . . . an' black ain't.

Hence the paraconcept addresses this double bind. And struggle needs to be had to reckon with this double bind. That bind is the necessity of refusing the premises on which the Negro, as a subject, rests and to not disregard the Negro, as subject, precisely because the historical trajectory of that subject is consequential. Forgive me now for conveying a lengthy passage from Chandler that illustrates this matter pristinely:

Study Notes," *Darkmatter* (blog), September 29, 2015, http://www.darkmatter101.org/site/2015/09/29/the-movement-of-black-thought-study-notes/.

It is thus that in the presupposition of such a replete position, this critique seems unable to recognize in the *historical situation* of the African American the most mundane of circumstances: that there is not now nor has there ever been a free zone or quiet place from which the discourse of so-called Africanist figures, intellectuals, writers, thinkers, or scholars might issue. And this can be shown to be the case in general. Such discourse always emerges in a context and is both a response and a call. In this specific instance, it emerges in a cacophony of enunciation that marks the inception of discourses of the "African" and the "Negro" in the modern period in the sixteenth century. At center of this cacophony was a question about what we now often call identity and forms of identification. On the surface, its proclaimed face, it was a discourse about the status of a putative Negro subject: political, legal, moral, philosophical, literary, theological, and so on. On its other, and hidden, face, was a question about the status of a putative European subject (subsequently understood as an omnibus figure of the "White"), the presumptive answer to which served as ground, organizing in a hierarchy the schema of this discourse, and determining the historically supraordinate elaboration of this general question. This hidden surface, as ground and reference of identification, along with the exposed surface that showed forth as a question about "Negro" identity, must be continually desedimented, scrutinized, and re-figured in their relation. It is the status of the identity that takes its stand in the shadows, or the system that it supposedly inaugurates, that is so often assumed in the de-essentializing projects that remain perennially afoot in African American and African diasporic studies. Or, if this "European" or "European American," or later "White," subject (presumptively understood as a simple whole despite its remarkable "internal" heterogeneity), or the system presumed to originate with it, is not simply assumed, the necessity, rigor, patience, and fecundity of antecedent Africanist discourses, as they have negotiated a certain *economy*, one within which such discourses (antecedent and contemporary, diasporic and continental) function, is too easily diminished, if not outright denied, in the perennial de-essentializing critique of the immediately past and present intellectual generations. (14–15, emphasis original)

The discourse of the Negro never comes from a place of sequestered quietude or freeness from all the surrounding static;

it does not, and has never, come from one writing, as it were, in "a room of one's own," taking, as many others have done, Virginia Woolf to task on her white feminine solipsism. That which erupts from the Negro as paraontological desedimentation works doubly as a response and a call: it works as an impure injection into the pervading white supremacy and as a transitive, anoriginary beckoning toward life unbounded by the ontological—which is to say, the white, cis, male, Western—dictates organizing life and livability. As the discourse of the Africanist figure arose, on one reading, in the cacophony of attempts to enunciate identificatory difference as a way to gain steam in promoting different conceptions of life for those who indexed the "ancient volcano," paraontological life, this discourse took on the identificatory project as well. Thus the Negro "subject" was given over to onto-epistemic criteria. This must be noted and, to an extent, an extent that is still up for debate and will likely always be nebulous, heeded. Too, however, the "European" or "White" subject (neither of which Chandler believes exists as such) organized the very ground of ontology, and the question of the subject, any iteration of the subject—whether Negro or non-Western or what have you—is always a reiterative process of the foundational subject ("European" or "White") and its logics for subjecthood proper. The white subject is the ground allowing all notions of "subject" to come forth, no matter how "black" it might be. This ground must be displaced, and the name Chandler gives for that displacement is the Negro, that figurative instantiation of desedimentation. Chandler is not arguing for simply a nonessentialist or anti-essentialist project, as such projects always presume the immutability and transparency of the ligaments of the ontological identificatory project without questioning, desedimenting, its grounds. Taking the Negro as a paraontological force, then, is the avenue by which we proceed toward unseating the grounds without assuming the immutability and transparency of the grounds that gave rise to the figure that permits us to unseat those grounds.

This is a project with deeply gendered resonances. The insistences on purity and ultimate grounds are the same insistences that seek to invalidate the livability of trans and gender nonnormative life. "Biological sex" and the gender binary are those pure, ultimate grounds that trans, prefixally and analytically and corporeally, originarily displaces, acts as exorbitant to. One must not, then, simply submit that there is such an identifiable, transparently knowable entity called a trans subject, nor submit that trans subjects do not really exist and bear no unique relationship to the process of ontologization. What, then, are we to do? While the phenomenological gendered experiences of trans people are not to be discarded, which would risk reifying the gendered ontology that orchestrates transantagonism, it can be said that trans as a prefixal indexation of gender desedimentation is precisely the working-on and undoing-of the organizing frame of the gender binary, necessary to be taken up by anyone making a practice—which is to say working toward a subjectivity—of dislodging the violence of ontology, of which the gender binary, biological essentialism and determination, and anatomical overdetermination are deeply constitutive. "Trans" is a figuration that is mapped onto certain subjective formations and modalities that "exist" by way of its effects on predominating onto-logics, yet those effects index that which precisely cannot exist within those logics, that which implies a life and livability not of this world.

I want to proffer a certain understanding of the trans or transness as a paraontological gesture. This is a proffering gaining its heft not only on indication of elision, a move that almost goes without saying and is, quite frankly, grossly lacking in revelation. Trans as bearing a paraontological residue, as it were, is a testament to the fact that other words besides "the Negro" or "African

American" can and *must* be used, that these other words do not replace or displace the efficacy of words that are already used (e.g., Negro), and that these words add genuine depth to what is being spoken of. Trans, then, like the X and the Negro and African American and blackness, must be thought alongside them, for they reference how and where desedimentation is taking place. Trans "converge[s] in an irreducible way" with the Negro, and when Fred Moten in his conversation with Wu Tsang says that "there are other words that one could use, but none of those words is replaceable. Not only are they not replaceable, they are not substitutable," he is speaking to the potency of trans as doing the work, or indexing the impulse of impurity, of what Chandler is indexing to the Negro as paraontological.[13] I emphasize the necessity of speaking to gender and the rending of its cohesion—that is, the trans/gender—because ontology is given over to readers of Chandler's text as an encompassing terrain of organization and coherence. And it organizes and coheres by way of what Chandler insists on calling racial distinction (not "race," Chandler always putting "race" in quotes). I cannot help but insist, too, on the gender binary as analogical to "racial distinction," irreducibly, because gender, like it seems Chandler implies with racial distinction's role in modernity organizing itself around racial taxonomies, "is also an administrative or bureaucratic structure for the management of sexual difference and reproductivecapacity."[14] The field of ontology is vehicularized

13. Fred Moten and Wu Tsang, "All Terror, All Beauty: Wu Tsang and Fred Moten in Conversation," in *Trap Door: Trans Cultural Production and the Politics of Visibility*, ed. Tourmaline, Eric A. Stanley, and Johanna Burton (Cambridge, Mass.: MIT Press, 2017), 347, 344.

14. Susan Stryker and Aren Z. Aizura, "Introduction: Transgender Studies 2.0," in *The Transgender Studies Reader 2*, ed. Susan Stryker and Aren Z. Aizura (New York: Routledge, 2013), 8.

in substantive part by gender as a *necessary and nonnegotiable* constituent of ontological status.

Hence, if the counterproject is to desediment the ground on which ontology gains its efficacy, and if the Negro is one name for that desedimentary project, another name for that, not reducible to the Negro but vital also to name, is *trans*. By way of Mel Y. Chen's definition, "*trans* is not as a linear space of mediation between two monolithic, autonomous poles, as for example 'female' and 'male'"—and this is the ontological function, a gestural fixity begotten by linearity, binarism, and homogeneity—"rather, *trans* is conceived of as more emergent than determinate, intervening with other categories in a richly intersectional space. . . . Rather than a substantive core such as a noun, I wish to highlight a *prefixal* 'trans-' not preliminarily limited to gender." They go on to remark that this is a "different form of trans-," one that does not evacuate the gendered valences of it or the affective registers it accrues around and through people of transgender experience. Trans, on Chen's account, is asserted as a "complex, multi-factored cultural contingency of transgendered actualizations [which] affirm that gender is omnipresent, though I am suggesting that it is rarely monolithically masculine or feminine."[15] Gender's omnipresence marks it as a fundamentally ontological predicate, making any effort to desediment ontology's hold one that necessarily attends to gender. This attention is not to be one that simply looks to "women's experience" or incorporates the perspectives of transgender people; it is a gender binaristic eruption—a transness that speaks the language of gender abolition.

15. Mel Y. Chen, "Animals without Genitals: Race and Transsubstantiation," in Stryker and Aizura, *Transgender Studies Reader 2*, 173, emphasis original.

Between

> To be named—even when the namer is godlike and
> blissful—perhaps always remains an intimation
> of mourning.
>
> —WALTER BENJAMIN, *"On Language as Such and on the
> Language of Man"*

CHANDLER GOES ON AT LENGTH about one word, the first word
of Du Bois's *Souls*: "Between." *Between* is incommensurate with
all that it is thought to name, so it may only be allusive of what
exceeds naming and nameability.[1] Chandler is reading Du Bois's

1. I got into a bit of a debate, with beloved colleagues and with
no hint of malice though, about naming. I was being pressed on my
rejection of the possibility of salvation in naming, being told that finding
new names might be a more ethical gesture because, indeed, how can
one live without a name? How can we say no to naming when there are
people who have insisted on inscribing their names into monuments as
an ethical gesture not only to never forget but also to know, now, for the
first time? It seems to me that, still, to desire one's name on the historical
ledger is to reinscribe the logic that one must be bestowed legibility and
thus livability *in a certain conception of life that is not the only conception
of life* by power. I am reminded of Lamonda Horton-Stallings who, in
Mutha' Is Half a Word, writes of the "(un)naming" Kimberly Benston
asserts people like Malcolm X and Ralph Ellison's Invisible Man took
up, a refusal of a name in order to name later or name, as it were, with
black accoutrements, and what she understood as a more radical black
feminist "unnaming": a practice she thinks in the context of gender that
might be generalized as "a process of unranking and challenging gender

"between" as a paleonymic term, a terminological rendering he gets from Derrida that means a new usage of an old word, a working and reworking with remnants that ultimately escape or destroy the word being used. Paleonomy, in other words, is a usage of "the Negro" where "emphasizing the predicative trait within the old name (i.e., 'the Negro') defines the 'unthought structural possibility' of that concept, designating it as the 'X' that remains to be theorized."[2] Du Bois's opening sentence brings about the problem of presence and the assumption of selfsameness. Because the relationship between "me" and "the other" dislodges both from a stable and oppositional boundedness, mimicked by "between" and "and," this throws the very question of selfsameness, of being, into question. This throwing into question *between* precipitates is the problem: the problem the root word of *problematic,* as the Negro is the general and generalized problematic for ontological grounds and pure being; and, too, the interrogative embedded in the titular problem of Chandler's text, the introductory interrogative "Problem?" of the present meditation.

He finds in the moment of the LA riots, which is no singular and isolated moment but a moment begotten by a series of other moments, reason for pause. The riots, sparked by the brutaliz-

---

[and perhaps subjectivity as such] through a manipulation of language to elide the troubles and violations of language in the West," an "interrupt[ion of] the subjective fictions of skin color, ovaries, uterus, and so on." Devoid of the parenthetical coding, Stallings's black feminist unnaming theorizes "a subject's willful, infinite, multiple, and continuous process of defying classification/naming." LaMonda Horton-Stallings, *Mutha' Is Half a Word: Intersections of Folklore, Vernacular, Myth, and Queerness in Black Female Culture* (Columbus: Ohio State University Press, 2007), 34–35, 38.

2. Barnor Hesse, "Of Race: The Exorbitant Du Bois," *Small Axe* 20, no. 2 (2016): 16, https://doi.org/10.1215/07990537-3626728.

ing of Rodney King in 1991, are the culmination of violence. A violence not confined to a singular moment but an inaugurative violence that has constituted the very conditioning ground that gave King over to the brutalization of police batons. The violence repeats and does not end, because King was violated before and after he was violated. And yet "we reach a limit," Chandler notes. "We cannot know, we cannot (only) name, here, in this domain" (1). This domain is one that is uninhabitable to the radical alternative to which we owe our allegiance. To name only in this domain—which might be to say, simply, to name—limits our (para)ontological breadth. Epistemic curtailment is inevitable when this domain is the only one in which knowledge is deemed knowledge as such. Importantly, Chandler's precision does not refuse this domain in its entirety, the domain with which we are accustomed, as if there have not always been clandestine and underground modes of living the desired radical alternative. We cannot "(only)" know and name here, so it is necessary that we continue to know and name here, but in a way that is perpetually moving toward, in the final instance, knowing and naming elsewhere. That elsewhere is in the between.

What does it mean to know and name in the between? Language and knowledge break down, and in the breaking down is where different kinds of names and knowledge arise, names and knowledge that might not be, indeed cannot be, properly called names and knowledge. The between cannot even be properly called a "place." The preposition is one that does not denote a locatable space as prepositions should; it marks movement in the nonlocatable and indeterminate space between poles—between, if you will, a binary of two referents. *Between,* in other words, inflects a movement between poles, binaristically oppositional poles that ooze so much with a connotative sex/gender binary. *Between,* in one sense, marks trans movement. Residing in the interstices of the poles is, in a sense, a death sentence—a willing obliteration of one's ontological foundation. A death sentence that permits the pursuit of another kind of life, life in the *interregnum,* those trans and transversal "moments . . . *between* the regime of what was and the promise of what might be."[3]

And here we begin to get at the figure of the X, as one of its definitions is in fact the figure's use as a mark of obliteration. The crossed out and X'ed out is the erased, the expurgation from grammatical dictates of syntactical existence between nounal poles and the agency of verbs. Too, then, the figure of the X carries with it a kind of figurative somethingness not of the determinant poles. I would propose that in the between is where X lives, its problematizing Negroness and troubling of gender wrapped up in this betweenness. The troubling of gender and thought is garnered not from a direct challenge to the extant poles determining thought and (binary) gender but from opting out of the logic; residence in the between, that nonlocatable nonspace, is a more fundamental and radical refusal of the poles firmly entrenched. The X, like "between," then figures as the authorization of "movement of an oppositional logic and a reading of it as radical," a moving radicality that ultimately inscribes the X as a designation for that "punctual rhythm of an en medias res inauguration" (4).

Between is a "word" in the text, or alternatively a *word.* There is such an emphasis on between's wordness, an emphasis that is not incidental. Chandler, in writing that between is a "word" or *word,* is looking to make a distinction. We reference something that we may not truly be able to reference when we say "between." "Between" is not the thing itself, a thing that may in

3. Hil Malatino, "Future Fatigue: Trans Intimacies and Trans Presents (or How to Survive the Interregnum)," *TSQ: Transgender Studies Quarterly* 6, no. 4 (2019): 644, emphasis added, https://doi.org/10.1215/23289252-7771796.

fact not be a thing but a force or process, or spatiality, unable to be delimited lexically. As a "word," between is more than a string of letters with a definition; as a *word,* between is being distinguished from the thing that cannot be named but is nonetheless usefully named in order to know it is something that exceeds its nominative. I will be speaking of the thing captivated, not captured, by the "word" and *word* between—and this is to say that I'll be speaking of *between,* my notation of this—as that is what bears the generative relation to the Negro and the trans; that is the problematizing rejoinder to ontology.

Between is "the disruptive and desedimenting movement" (9) Chandler writes as "between," with scare quotes. The preeminent utility in Du Bois's oeuvre and in the first word of *Souls* is what it announces, at least for Chandler, and, I've decided, for my purposes as well: it announces, "in radical fashion," a "preoccupation and making trembling of the logic *of being*" (9, emphasis original). This making trembling is a desedimentary move, a loosening of the hold being has on ontological grounds. *Between* connotes, and tries but fails to name, this making trembling, this reverberatory and quaking mutability fissuring the bastion of ontology. Important to note is that *it* doesn't tremble; it *makes tremble,* a distinction expressive of the very movement desedimentation and, too, the Negro and the trans characterize. Being has a logic that allows it not only to be legible as being but also to exist as being, a logic that is alogicized by *between* and Du Bois's inauguration of *Souls* with that "word" and *word. Between* makes impure the purity of being's logic by making tremble—perhaps as verb *and* noun, inasmuch as *between* connotes that which bears the status of the tremble, of trembling, of a kind of, if you will, tremblation.

Via Du Bois, *between* does something different: it disrupts any notion of boundary, of an identifiable inside and outside. It is a syntactical movement with (para)ontological ramifications, that of a dissipation of the limits imposed from without, and also, maybe, from within. *Between,* when met with inside/outside, with strict—or any—limits and delimitations, is irreverent. Inside and outside imply location and locatedness. *Between* is nonlocatable, an impure spatiality.

Taken as radical oppositional logic, betweenness poses a tremendous problem: its betweenness. Its problematics rest in itself, its existence in a nonspace that is disallowed from existence insofar as the poles between which betweenness is (un)situated determine existence. It poses its own logic by finding livability in the nonsanctioned. To *move* in the between, which is to say to dwell in betweenness, since inhabiting betweenness is to not "be" in a locatable spot and thus to be moving inasmuch as movement is the refusal of "being in" one gridlocked vector, proposes a radical kind of logic. It is another logic and an other logic in subversion of that which sustains the syntactical and grammatical integrity of the poles. As indexical of this, X subsequently becomes the "punctual rhythm" that conditions ontological betweenness, an ontology that is more accurately a paraontology, or further still, a negaontology—ontology that cannot abide ontological tenets and thus lives, exists, be's in the evacuated bowels of ontological apparatuses; negaontology, tentatively, as being without ontology. This rhythmic punctuality begins in the middle. Beginning in the middle, it inaugurates those proximal to X's subjective force into this middle—the between—and they become through subjectivity in that middle radical logic of opposition. X inaugurates another kind of subjectivity by way of a beginning in the middle, opposing teleologics.

Or perhaps "begin" is a misnomer. To begin inhabits a temporal frame of linearity that belies the fundamental problematics the X and its betweenness set forth. But Chandler provides more suitable language in the very title of his opening chapter: "Anacrusis." The *anacrusis,* the titular opening of Chandler's text and, semantically, the preceding striking up or prelude to the beginning of a verse of prose or music—which is to say, the anoriginal transitivity, the nothingness and dispersive indistinction upon which sedimented meaning rests—is language that befits the anoriginality toward which the X is striving. Saidiya Hartman has labeled Chandler's use of anacrusis "the expectant music of the before," his "step-by-step guide to paraontology."[4] Anacrusis is a precursory setting in motion, but one that has always already been occurring in ways that prove unintelligible to extant logics of measurement. The anacrusis gives us a timid glimpse into that which happens, and is always already happening, before the onset of categorizing regimes, and it is there where the radical alternative force finds a definitional solace. To think of the X in intimate proximity to anacrusis, we come to get at X's betweenity, its displacing anoriginality, its preceding problematic, its evasive previousness that exceeds the obsession with a beginning natality.

Racially echoing that famous Du Boisian question, I want to query how the Negro problem resounds pervasively, putting pressure on racialized identification and contemporary thought; I want to query, too, what it might mean for the trans/gender problem to resound pervasively, to ask if those of trans experience are problem people—we might say, a blackened gender insofar as blackness indexes a problematic, *the* problematic, given in referential overlapping relation with nonnormative/trans genders. Then it can be argued that the "double question," the displacing question Chandler highlights, circulates around the very meaning, the very effects, of the Negro problem and the (trans)gender problem. But, let me back up, if only to get us to move ever more forward.

---

4. Saidiya Hartman, "Liner Notes for the Riot," *E-Flux* 105 (2019), https://www.e-flux.com/journal/105/302565/liner-notes-for-the-riot/.

The fragmentary text that is of concern in *X—the Problem of the Negro as a Problem for Thought* is Du Bois's *The Souls of Black Folk,* and concerning the first chapter of Chandler's book is the very first word of Du Bois's. One word that inaugurates, that unsettles, so much: Between. Many of you know the passage already, perhaps committed it to memory, able to spew its gorgeous discursive tunes, as they say, by heart. "Between me and the other world there is ever an unasked question," Du Bois writes.

> Unasked by some through feelings of delicacy; by others through the difficulty of rightly framing it. All nevertheless, flutter round it. They approach me in a half-hesitant sort of way, eye me curiously or compassionately, and then, instead of saying directly, How does it feel to be a problem? they say, I know an excellent colored man in my town; or I fought at Mechanicsville; or, Do not these Southern outrages make your blood boil? At these I smile, or am interested, or reduce the boiling to a simmer, as the occasion may require. To the real question, How does it feel to be a problem? I answer seldom a word.

This serves as an opening for Chandler, an opening into the fracturous space of the between, a space that demands an inhabitation precisely because it asks to be inhabited yet does not appear habitable. Between's radicality stems from its positioning as seeming to stabilize and give coherence to what follows ("me and the other . . .") yet lacking in predication—there is no "There is" or "There" or "In" preceding the word "Between," making it its own position, unmoored in a no-place, a prepositional referent without a reference—and thus offering a disjointed groove from which to usher in "the radical possibility of this other logic" (4).

This other logic, indeed an Other logic or logic not-as-such, errs away from the stabilizing of poles and opts for the instability and uncertainty of the very position that acts more as a non-position. Du Bois's "Between" gives a grounding for the other logic the Negro, via the X, operates on, but reading in Du Bois's "Between" a riff on the word, as *betweenity* in the trans poetic language of Meg Day, is a way to think through the noted gender troubling of the trans and nonbinary that happen precisely *between* the dimorphic male and female, man and woman.[5] I wish to say more here, and hope I succeed in this problematic and problematizing endeavor, than simply that trans people might also make recourse to the Du Boisian and, hence, racial language. Though surely this is partly my aim, to end here is not enough. The task at hand is, as I've said, to note that those given to trans experience may, too, make use of and find home in this language shrouded by the vector of blackness; it is also, I posit, to uncover how the semantic, logical, and conceptual bedrock that underpins ontological status is displaced by the desedimentary logics of the paraontological, to which the trans—the gender nonnormative, the nonbinary—lays claim due to its potency under the heading of deregulation, unmooring, and a kind of deconstruction. Negro problematics are BFFs with gender problematics.

Being problematic in this sense is to trouble, by way of a lack of adherence to the holds that would allow ontology to grasp, domesticating problems, taming them into nonproblems at best and answers, resolved things, at worst. The problematic Du Bois initiates is via the between, as *between* cannot be placed at the poles that would allow knowability and emplotment into the ontological grid. There is a between that is more than the word—it

5. Meg Day, "Poetics Statement," in *Troubling the Line: Trans and Genderqueer Poetry and Poetics,* ed. T. C. Tolbert and Trace Peterson (Callicoon, N.Y.: Nightboat Books, 2013), 387. Day describes this as "existing between identities & among identities and as always shifting identities," culminating in a "badass body of betweenity."

is the preceding "ancient volcano" (4) that presents the possibility for radicality by implying but disavowing predication. The predication is a grounding, a stable one, that *between* refuses, makes impure, makes tremble. Via Du Bois's style, *between* is no longer a thing that sets up an oppositional logic but a disorganized incoherence, a perpetual movement of concealment of finalized meaning, a constant suspension permitting an instability, a refusal of the poles endemic to an opposition, a binary—*between* as disorganizing the coherence of a binary, making it, too, a trans sensibility. Gender is organized by, made coherent through, a fundamental and biologized binary that *between* unfixes. Where Du Bois's between spatializes the relation between "me [Du Bois] and the other . . . ," or between as indexical of the Negro problem, the problematic Negro, between also must be taken to imply a betweenity extant within Du Bois's between, as a synecdoche for blackness. That is, Du Bois is not the ground of the Negro; the Negro, as an ungrounded ground, is fractured along the lines of, and does the fracturing of the lines of, gender. There is movement occurring even at the level of the Negro, a movement of gender, a problematizing of gender, which is to say the transness of the between.

Let me say this again, in another way, explicitly. The Negro gives us gender as a problem first for the Negro and then, in a generalizing move of which Chandler is fond, for being. (I might also drop the temporal qualifier and say simply that the Negro is coeval with trans/gender as a problem.) As C. Riley Snorton explained, "blackness, [i]s a condition of possibility that made transness conceivable in the twilight of formal slavery," which is to conclude that "gender for the black and blackened takes on an anagrammatical quality, subject to reiterative rearrangement." Or, citing Lamonda Horton-Stallings's transaesthetics, which Snorton also makes use of and which dovetail with the *funk* of blackness, blackness "disturb[s] forms, biological and otherwise."[6] If the Negro-cum-blackness anagrammaticalizes gender by definition, and if grammatical gender is gender as such—the grammar being ontological predication—and, further still, if blackness makes transness possible in the era of Western enslavement, there is an inextricable relationship between the Negro and the trans, such that the Negro as a problem cannot be spoken of, cannot do its problematizing, without a meditation on how it necessitates a problem for and of gender.

6. Snorton, *Black on Both Sides,* 135–36; see also LaMonda Horton-Stallings, *Funk the Erotic: Transaesthetics and Black Sexual Cultures* (Urbana: University of Illinois Press, 2015).

The Interminable Figure of the X

> The black chant she hears is old and new to her. She is
> unmoored. She is ungendered.
>
> —FRED MOTEN, *"Blackness and Nothingness (Mysticism in the
> Flesh)"*

IMPORTANTLY, "X" might be read as a Derridean repackaging
with a difference—or, if you will, with a *différance*. If *différance*
is a movement of the trace and instantiation of the impossibility
of origin and a shattering of cultist identitarianism, X proceeds
along these routes as well. X is not "simply nothing (or, rather,
not absence)" (77); X is the trace of a movement for which we
are always too late, a movement of displacement, a movement
toward a certain rupture of the thing that permits sedimentation.
X's utility comes in its ability to mark an absence, to reference a
non-thing, placing it in the *between,* as discussed in the previous
chapter: X is a thing that is not a *thing.* Like the Negro, and I
would insist on the addition of the trans and gender nonnormative, X is a figural figure, yet not a figure proper (101); it marks a
difficulty posed to the identificatory, the ontological, imposition.

But whence does this niggling little letter that is so much more
than a letter come? The letter *X* has a rather shifty history. It
has morphed like other letters and phonemes, of course, but its
etymological trajectory proves particularly useful in excavating
the possibility of a link to contemporary understandings of nonnormative modes of existence.

X was originally used by the Phoenicians as a representative of the hard consonant /s/ sound *(samekh)*, which the Greeks later borrowed around 900 B.C.E. and named "Chi." The Greeks then used this letter to simplify the digraphic /ks/ sounds, a sound pervasive in western Greece. Subsequently, the Romans adopted the /x/ sound from the Chalcidian alphabetic system, borrowing the "Chi" symbol, and wrote it as two diagonally crossed strokes (what we might understand today as an *X*). Thus, in short, the Romans took the /x/ sound from the Chalcidian alphabet, combined it with the diagonally stroked "Chi" symbol from the Greeks, and that confluence begot the letter *X* as we know it. Now, *X* is an especially phonetically volatile letter. It can be written to announce a voiceless velar fricative (your common /ks/ sound), a /gz/ sound exemplified in words like "auxiliary," or the /z/ sound, as in "xylophone," and it can be soundless, as in "faux."

In excess of strict syntactic and semantic shifts and meanings of "X," it has also taken on broader social meanings that open up avenues of thought, or rather, that problematize thought. The *X*-shaped Phoenician "Taw" symbol has roots in Old Testament scriptures as a mark to be borne in order to avoid being smitten by the angel of death. It was a signifier of divinely chosen life. Too, it has marked the location of unknown variables (X marks the spot); it has acted itself as the unknown variable (as in mathematical *x* variables, or more loosely in what has been deemed the "X-factor") and has denoted the obliteration of typed script. "X" has long marked error, too, to which any teacher with a red pen can attest. Additionally, it marks relationality, or how a preceding quantity relates to the subsequent one, as in measurements (e.g., 2 × 4). And lastly, though there are likely others that escape this brief enumeration, *X*s have been used to signify kisses, with its accompanying *O* for hugs, in friendly and romantic missives.

Most apropos for my concerns, however, is perhaps X's racialized and chromosomal inflections. X has come to imply, in the afterlife of U.S. enslavement of African-descended peoples, a marker of absence for an unknown Africanic surname. A referent to that locus of blackness, that "dark continent," X signifies a type of nothingness insofar as such a nothingness indexes both the epithetic and racist conception of Africa as producing nothing of intellectual and cultural value as well as the no-thingness the name blackness comes to stand in for: an absolute dispersal of generativity, what Amaryah S. Armstrong would understand as blackness in its exuding of an abundant multiplicity, or what Claire Colebrook would understand as a transitivity in its not-yet-differentiated potentiality to give rise to distinction.[1] Many ex-slaves in the late nineteenth century and African-descended people in the twentieth and twenty-first centuries who wished to supplant their "slave names" took to declaring their last name as, simply, "X." The mark, the "remainder" (111), that is, the X is a kind of surplus, referential of "the interminable figure" (176). As interminable, the X is perennially open-ended. An endlessness of the X is indicative of an ongoing mutability and processual alteration, a never-being-closed or finished. This open-endlessness, if you will, excites the Negro and the trans, as the X names the unnamed, the blessed loss of namedness; this open-endless X, to reactivate contextually differently Cameron Awkward-Rich's "[Black Feeling]," is "a room where things go / to lose their names," becoming "[ ]."[2] The letter, then, comes to stand in for an unnameable blackness that was lost or stolen—a trans experience, I want to assert briefly, in that "to feel black

1. Amaryah Shaye, "Refusing to Reconcile, Part 2," *WIT* (blog), February 16, 2014, https://womenintheology.org/2014/02/16/refusing-to-reconcile-part-2/; Claire Colebrook, "What Is It Like to Be a Human?," *Transgender Studies Quarterly* 2, no. 2 (2015): 227–43.

2. Cameron Awkward-Rich, *Dispatch: Poems* (New York: Persea, 2019), 67.

in the diaspora," which brings with it a necessary relation to the Middle Passage and histories of forced captivity and cultural theft, "might be a trans experience," and also in that *stealing the body back* inflects a trans/gender self-determinative mode of existence—and this unnameable blackness is, put differently, the figure of the Negro as the figure of the X.[3] To quote Chandler:

> We can recall that X of the shuttling signature that remains of the unnamed and unnameable Negro or African American slaves of the four centuries up to the nineteenth, only iconically recollected at the juncture of emancipation when the ex-slave soon to become the so-called freedman [*sic*], could mark only X for a name, to indicate or proclaim her, or his, status. (102)

Surely the very idea of race marks our history and, indeed, marks us ontologically to the extent that we might not even be able to become subjects (now) without recourse to that structuration. Nevertheless, Du Bois's color-line problem and the extant racist structures and attitudes are in fact a *response,* Chandler notes, to a more originary process of centrifuge and dispersal. It is *that* originary thing to which structures of categorization respond that occupies the figure of the X—that unknown factor of centrifuge and dispersal—and which occupies the more general possibility to which the problematizing analytics of blackness and transness give rise. Of utmost concern is "the *problem* of the status of difference in general" (71, emphasis added), a difference that is mobilized for its problematics and presents the possibility of identification otherwise: an identification as a kind of disidentification. This concerns a radically different way of identifying, a radical way that puts pressure on the very means

---

3. Snorton, *Black on Both Sides,* 8; Jordy Rosenberg, "Trans/War Boy/Gender: The Primitive Accumulation of T," *Salvage* (blog), December 21, 2015, http://salvage.zone/in-print/trans-war-boy-gender/.

by which we come to subjectivate ourselves. Operation under the sign of race, or blackness, is indicative of a more general and fundamental question *of* difference and differentiation— the originary dispersal that is the black *and* trans of the matter.

As X relates to gender, it is a growing practice in places like Nepal, Pakistan, Bangladesh, Australia, New Zealand, Germany, Canada, and some states in the United States (Washington, Oregon, and California among them) to have X legally mark one's gendered relation to the State. The X in these cases is akin to what is being dubbed a "third gender," or sometimes (as in the case of Australia) akin to a "decline to state" status, but is on the whole meant to be a capacious signifier of all genders not exclusively "male" or "female" (if any genders in fact *are* exclusively locked on one side of the binary). As well, as conveyed by Joshua M. Ferguson, "in Japan today, *ekkusu-jendā* (X-gender) people identify as an intermediate gender. So-called third genders in China (*yinyang ren*), Samoa (*fa'afafine*), the Philippines (*bakla*), Thailand (*kathoey*), and Tonga (*fakaleiti*) have been documented."[4] X, too, has a chromosomal significance. The X chromosome—often the so-called female chromosome—renders the letter saturated with a kind of femininity or maternity, its affiliation with what is thought to be the "mother's" only chromosome making it hefty with gendered significatory power.[5] X's figuration as a "figural figure that is no figure," in Chandler's

4. Joshua M. Ferguson, *Me, Myself, They: Life beyond the Binary* (Toronto, Ont.: Anansi Press, 2019), 7–8.

5. It must be noted that the giving of an X chromosome does not mean that it was given by the "mother" or by a "woman." X chromosomes are present, of course, in cis men, but also in trans men, nonbinary people, and people with intersex conditions. Thus I mean not at all to imply the naturalness of the femininity and maternity often ascribed to the X chromosome, only to alert us to how the chromosome moves discursively throughout the social realm.

terms, is the marker of an absence, but a marker with an inherent lability. Such a lability is engendered by "a dispersal of forces" (or a transitivity) that, when speaking of paternity, continues to bear the mark of its figural effects. This Chandler circumstantially colloquializes, tellingly, "as the X of the chromosomal kind" (101–2).

Moreover, this chromosomal X and its circulation around questions of paternity, a paternity shrouded in lability that Chandler argues Du Bois's narrative has the ironic effect of desedimenting, bears the overall figurative problematic of the Negro as streamed through the X. It raises the critique of pure origins, which have not only the racial inflection Du Bois and Chandler point out (that is, in the context of Du Bois interrogating his mixed parentage) but also the gendered inflection residing in a general critique of when we might locate a coherent and uninterrupted—or unmixed—gendered origin, corporeal or chromosomal. The difficulty, which is to say the problematizing, the X poses, its racialized and gendered traces ever present, is one for Being's ground. The X's propulsion by the figure of the Negro and nonnormative gender allow for a fundamental interrogation of the historicized instantiations of these figures; they allow for a radical disintegrative interrogation of "the Negro," "the transgender," and ultimately "the human" in their saturative exorbitance of ontology—in their problematizing.

As a method of desedimented irreducible difference counterposing, or better, transposing—"the everyday act of becoming otherwise"; changing something into another form or a simultaneously destructive and generative "deviation that discomposes order" descriptive of transsexuality—the projected and imposed space of purity (on which ontology rests), X gets at a becoming other and becoming oneself.[6] Or, a becoming oneself

6. Eva Hayward, "Spiderwomen," in *Trap Door: Trans Cultural Production and the Politics of Visibilty*, ed. Reina Gossett, Eric A. Stanley, and Johanna Burton (Cambridge, Mass.: MIT Press, 2017), 255.

by way of the other; or, again, differently, a becoming other than oneself through the other that has been erected to buttress oneself, which is another way to say an unbecoming inasmuch as becoming is a departure from being. And being is X's ontological nemesis. There is no origin, we know. No bedrock foundation, no Aristotelian prime mover or first cause to which we can point, no Motherland housing our totality prior to some kind of corruption, no Eden. We are not in search of a totalizing whole, for which beingness is indexical. Our aim is the paraontological, a sort of originary impurity, which is no origin at all if origin is definitionally a pure, unperturbed beginning state. We are, and must be, impure from the start. Desedimentation, affixed to X's effects, revokes the sediment's license to stay here, grounded, as the ground. The ground's sediment has given us the way we are and must be. To proliferate desedimentation will require, then, another way.

And the figure of the X is a solicitation to view ourselves "in a radically *other* way" (111, emphasis original). If I may, this radically other way is necessarily bound up with the radical re-seeing of oneself, one's very subjectivity, that occurs in gender transition. Undergoing hormone replacement therapy and observing the gradual process of seeing one's facial features, one's chest, one's genitals, one's body hair shift and move, appear and disappear, can be construed as the emergence of a radically other self that is, paradoxically enough, a self that may have long been there. Gender transitioning is a conceptual ensemble that traffics in the realms of ideality and the corporeal, requiring an alteration in the apparatus of encountering self and others; thus it marks a slow-going other way in which one sees oneself as well as how one quite simply *sees,* how and from where one gains a perceptual purview. And this swings pendulously from the seeming benignity of, say, looking in the mirror over the course of the early stages of taking hormones, seeing oneself in another and an other way, to a more trepidatious looking, as in that conveyed by Miss Major Griffin-Gracy: "always paying attention to people coming past you and *how they look at you,* worrying that once they go behind you, they are going to turn around and come back at you," she says in a conversation with CeCe McDonald and Toshio Meronek. "So you learn to *look in reflections*—off of store windows, or windows on cars—just to be sure, because you never know."[7] In short, the radical other way of looking and, indeed, becoming solicited by the figure of the X is present in other realms of subject formation. These other realms, namely, gender—or what might be called such—are, too, constitutive of ontological grounds, the Negro and the trans desedimentative of them.

This framework bolsters my search for "something" that is "X": analytic patterns, processes of becoming, transformations, fault lines, and the problematics of the present. Illustrative of much of this, if I might be permitted a brief meditation on another text, is Claudia Milian's *LatinX.*[8] Milian is concerned with the history and reverberations of the phrase "Latinx," as the book's title implies, and she articulates this in ways that converge with my own discussion. Latinx serves not as a decided, delimited demographic or geographic; rather, it is indicative of an analytic itinerary working as a "speculative springboard" of indeterminacy. More than a mere gender-neutral neologism for "Latino/a" people, *Latinx* is descriptive of, indeed inaugurative

7. Miss Major Griffin-Gracy, CeCe McDonald, and Toshio Meronek, "Cautious Living: Black Trans Women and the Politics of Documentation," in Tourmaline, Stanley, and Burton, *Trap Door: Trans Cultural Production and the Politics of Visibility*, 27, emphasis added.

8. Claudia Milian, *LatinX* (Minneapolis: University of Minnesota Press, 2019), hereafter, because it concerns a decent chunk of the rest of the chapter, paginated in parentheses.

of and emergent through, a certain rupture in the implicit purity of the being of "Latin."

"The X," Milian writes, is "one that is falling through the Latin cracks—the spaces between the o's and the a's" (2). Where "o's" and "a's" signify the fortress of the gender binary, X falls through its cracks, fracturing the gender binary and, further, binaries by definition. It is an excessive little lexical figure, refusing to abide the grammatical syntax necessitated for certain kinds of legibility. Where the binary, indexed historically to both race (e.g., white/black) and what is called sex (e.g., male/female), has been cast pervasively as an organizing apparatus, the X in Latinx, and, too, the X as the figural figure of the nonfigure that is blackness synecdochalized as the Negro "complicates and makes space for discussions that do not solely rely on binary configurations" (2). Binary configurations are axiological configurations, configurations as such, casting a wide net over worldly inhabitation and relation. It can be contended, thus, that Latinx's "X" is a general problematic that speaks more broadly to subjectivity in general.

This general problematic signified by the X is present explicitly in Milian's short text as well as in its less conspicuous folds. She writes that "Xs are not a single body of ethnoracial, cultural, or gendered identification" (32), stating plainly that X is not a *specific* classification of ethnicity, race, or gender—and we might say the same, or something similar, about "Latinx" as well—but rather alluding to, stating a bit more implicitly, X's status as rupturative of identification itself, where identification means choosing from given options bestowed by normativity—X's status, in other words, as a blessed impurity in the pool of ontological purity. But that X is a general problematic, a generalized impurity in ontology and thus significatory of the process of subjectivation, is not a flattening, as Chandler implies, an implication he maybe had no other option than to make, as his itinerary was one hooked to racial distinction toward ontological generality. Looking to Milian's *LatinX* and gleaning from this a discussion of gender permits a way to discuss gender as what might be notated as a nongeneralizable generality. A discussion of X's gendered inflections is not meant to reduce X to a specific identificatory avenue, as if to say Chandler and those of his school—Hortense Spillers, Fred Moten, J. Kameron Carter, Sarah Jane Cervenak, and others—problematically elide the import of, say, "women." This discussion, as I've said and will further say elsewhere, drawing on Spillers, is a way to articulate X as a problem for gender via an intentional effort, a concerted "trying to go through gender to get to something wider."[9] X is linked inextricably to gender as a chief site of problematizing because gender is a chief vector of establishing ontology. And X bears a gendered potency via the chromosomal and the gender-neutral, and nonbinary in particular, that cannot be overlooked.

Xs are assemblages of unknowns, or indeterminates, or faults, or dissemblances, or irreducible noncommunicabilities. The X engenders new and other political deployments unable, perhaps, to be ensnared by capturative tendrils. Interestingly, "X" as a nonreferent to a thing that is maybe not a thing in the typical sense straddles the paradox; that is, we describe not an extant thing, as such a thing would have to abide the logics of legibility and be given an ontic form, provisional as it may be. But in giving that non-thing the language of the X, we in a sense give it over to legibility, literally inscribing it. Hence, X marks a captivation that skirts but alludes to captivity—X as captivating but not capturative. It is the path we travel to get to pathlessness.

9. Spillers et al., "'Whatcha Gonna Do?': Revisiting 'Mama's Baby, Papa's Maybe: An American Grammar Book': A Conversation with Hortense Spillers, Saidiya Hartman, Farah Jasmine Griffin, Shelly Eversley, & Jennifer L. Morgan," *Women's Studies Quarterly* 35, no. 1/2 (2007): 304.

X, Milian writes, is our "trajectory," but, at the same exact time, in its multiplicative "numerosities," as Milian beautifully and succinctly entitles her concluding chapter, "X [i]s ____."

Most illuminatively for my purposes is a select passage from *LatinX*. Milian writes,

> I gather what is available at this moment, the X, taking LatinX's "X" as a fruitful incitation, contemplation, and speculation—an urgent hermeneutic necessity for today. Its unifying problematic and interpretable features are linked by crises of the moment: "breaking" news and everyday events, instability, and projected catastrophic disasters and loss, as well as rapid change and disorientation that analytically put us to work. (5)

X is here described as an urgent hermeneutic, which is to say a figurative figure; X is a "problematic" linked to various kinds of crisis. X mobilizes crisis and serves as a marker for crisis. It incites, perturbs. An analytic for these crises, X, Milian shows, implies a disorientation that puts things to work. In this sense it dovetails seamlessly with Kai M. Green's articulation of what they understand as the work of "trans*." As Green puts it, one of the "multiple registers" on which trans* is deployed is as "a reading practice that might help readers gain a reorientation to orientation."[10] The referential overlap between X and trans, or "trans*," is precisely what I am thinking as Chandler's X-as-Negro as a problem, or problematizing analytic, of and for gender. The X of Latinx, Milian notes, is an orientational matter for thought, and she cites Chandler explicitly (39). Dexterously, she thinks the X in a Chandlerian vein in the same context as a nongeneralizable generality of gender, indexing her discussion to Spanish as a gendered Romance language that we can, *from there,*

---

10. Kai M. Green, "Troubling the Waters: Mobilizing a Trans* Analytic," in *No Tea, No Shade: New Writings in Black Queer Studies,* ed. E. Patrick Johnson (Durham, N.C.: Duke University Press, 2016), 67.

from that gendered specificity, begin to think as an unknowable and beyond-knowable rhetorical maneuver. As an unclassifiable indexation, as it were. We get to that through and after gender. X in Milian's formulation is a disorientation; trans* in Green's account is a reorientation to orientation, or a disorientation to get to another kind of—an other logic for—how we are oriented; Chandler's X-as-Negro is a figure of this other logic that fundamentally disturbs ontology and pure being, or the very parameters by which we are oriented to and as ourselves. The problem of the Negro, the X, is a problem for, and by way of, gender.

In the end, the X is a significatory implicative of possibilities on the horizon. But it is more than merely to come; the X, its *gendered* valences reveal, unlike what Chandler finds through the valences that supervene upon racial distinctions, is already doing this significatory work as it is a possibility already here in, say, the Latin*x* and the chromosomally portentous X. The simplicity of the X as a referent for the problem of the Negro as a problem for thought—a "thought" that foundations metaphysics and ontology as well as the traditional philosophical baggage they bear—must not overshadow its reference of the problematics that inhere in and as, too, gender.

Hacked X

... the unintelligible trans that plays with gender and
understands transness as transcendence.

—KRIZIA PUIG, *"The TransAlien Manifesto: Future Love(s),
Sex Tech, and My Efforts to Re-member Your Embrace"*

THE "THING" THAT PRECEDES something like the LA riots, the
thing to which the riots respond—a long-occurring nothing-
newness that subtends life as an ongoing violence—is what
Chandler calls the *"disaster"* (1, emphasis original). The disas-
ter is the thing that permits the legibility and possibility of the
Rodney King beating, the shooting of Itali Marlowe and Atatiana
Jefferson. The disaster, though, need not be anything spectacular.
It often isn't. The disaster is something like racial distinction.
The disaster, too, is other subjective distinctions, which is, is not
the gender binary, too, a kind of disaster?

Problems do not exist in and of themselves. Problems do not
simply have an ontology that is self-evident outside of various
structures that pose this thing as, indeed, a problem. Problems
must problematize; within problems, as a noun, there is always
an agential verb—the doing and making of the problem that the
problem is said to be. If X indexes the Negro and (trans)gender
problem, X also signifies that these figures are not ontological
facts existent outside of other structures that deem them such;
they are verbs that do the work of problematizing. They serve
as problems for the purported unproblematic world in which

these problems are situated. They serve as problems for the pure. Thus, X's demarcation of error or wrongness, its indexation of the black Negro and nonnormative gender, demarcates, then, a refutation of Chandler's "project of purity" rooted not simply in "(. . . the superiority or supremacy of) a social subject understood as 'White' or (White) European'" (20) but also, I maintain, in the superiority of the presumed coherently gendered body, a gendered body predicated on its immersion in either pole of the gender binary—the trans, too, in Eva Hayward's terms, "as . . . meant to disturb *purification* practices."[1] There have long been problem people: the Negro problem concerned the heady question "What are we going to do with these freed Negroes"; the transgender problem, what perhaps can find roots in the gay problem insofar as "gaybashing" was not simply a reaction to sexual acts but also a violence stemming from the transgressive gender expression indexical, supposedly, of nonheterosexual sexual acts. So it becomes a matter of what problem people *do,* how purported problems are texturing their problematizing, a problematizing of which the Negro and the trans can be exemplars. Or rather, it precisely does not become a matter of anything inasmuch as these figurative problems, the Negro and the trans, produce exorbitances that exceed "all forms of being that truly matter" (23).

The Negro as figured through and as the X denotes a disruption, an "exorbitance" or "originary displacement," in Chandler's nomenclature. How, though, might the revelation of the introduction of *gender* to the U.S. lexicon bear on this? In the United States, "gender" was a sexological introduction meant to regulate unruly bodies, or bodies that did not adhere to the boundaries of the gender binary—"male" or "female." Not until the

1. Eva Hayward, "More Lessons from a Starfish: Prefixial Flesh and Transspeciated Selves," *Women's Studies Quarterly* 36, no. 3/4 (2008): 69, emphasis added.

early 1950s with the publication of John Money's dissertation, "Hermaphroditism: An Inquiry into the Nature of a Human Paradox," did the term "gender" begin to mark something closer to how we understand it today. For Money, though a controversial and vexing figure in the fields of intersex and trans studies for reasons that focus primarily on his surgical intervention on intersex children to make their genitals and bodies more aligned with normative genders, Money nonetheless used the term *gender* to describe not only a linguistic relation between words; gender became for the first time, at least pervasively, what a person is or could be, an ontological status conferred onto infants and fetuses that were presumed to persist unchangingly. Hence, questions that are now possible, like "What gender are you?" or "What is your gender?" were not really possible in the English language until post-Money and his discourse on "hermaphrodites."[2]

This is all to say, in short, that sex-cum-gender nonnormativity became a *disturbance* that needed to be "managed." The rending of gender normativity at the site of the infant with nonnormative genitals—and thus the projected future of gender nonconformity—was what brought *gender* as a term online. This constituted what Judith Butler has called a "deviant beginning," and thus gender "named a problem, an errancy or deviation, a failure to actualize the developmental norm in time. It exposed the fact that sex and gender do not always match, that the one does not mirror the other; that the one does not follow from the other. *Gender was not an identity, but the name for that very incommensurability.*"[3] This incommensurability, this inability to be expressed in common social subjective integers (e.g., "male,"

2. See Judith Butler, "Gender in Translation: Beyond Monolingualism," *PhiloSOPHIA* 9, no. 1 (2019): 12, https://doi.org/10.1353/phi.2019.0011.
3. Butler, 12–13, emphasis added.

"female"; "man," "woman"), gives gender and the nonnormativity it inaugurated or highlighted over to a sense of anoriginary displacement. If the figure of the "hermaphrodite" can be understood as a precursor to, or prefiguration of, a generalized sense of transness, then trans is marked by this incommensurability and thus primordial displacement. For "X" to be a marker of, among other things, a birth (non)gender or an intersex identification, which could accurately describe many of Money's patients, the X comes to stand in as a problem of gender—X-as-nonnormatively-gendered-subjects is a problem for thought, for the body.

Where Chandler reads in Du Bois's critique of race's ground an emphasis on the nonphysical, which implements a theorization of difference and differentiation as "undoubtedly based on the physical, but infinitely transcending them" (39), I read this maneuver alongside Puig and the epigraph that graces this chapter as an unintelligible transness and play, too, with gender transcendence, a play with gender to get to trans as a name for that Spillersian "something wider." So what comes next demands a bit of a swerve. A productive foray into the black feminist work of Denise Ferreira da Silva illuminates a potent avenue for thinking the X. Da Silva brings the mathematical to black feminism, theorizing Chandler's figure of the X as hacking—or breaching defenses set up to preserve the integrity of normative systems—gender. Bringing Hortense Spillers's female flesh ungendered to bear on Chandler's Negro, his X, da Silva hacks the X ("\X" as hacked X, ungendered or transed X) and uses \X as a device of confrontation to disrupt patriarchal forms and figurings. \X "explode[s] the male-form XY" and thus serves my purposes of illuminating how X as the figure of the Negro doubles, or polysemously singles, as a gender problematic.[4] Da Silva math-

4. Denise Ferreira da Silva, "Hacking the Subject: Black Feminism and Refusal beyond the Limits of Critique," *PhiloSOPHIA* 8, no. 1 (2018): 31.

ematically solves already known equations of biological repro-
duction, namely, sexually reproductive heterosexual cisgender
coupling and cisgender coupling without the "mother-wife."
But further, she deploys the hacked X as an experimentalizing
of these already known equations, concluding that hacking X—
problematizing systematicity and the normative tenets on which
proper racial and gendered logic rest to engender Man—leads
to a Kantian "Thing" unable to be apprehended by intuitional
forms or categories. Hacking the X leads to an excessive mode
of living that troubles existing logics and offers the potential for
forms of life other than current stultifying ones.

"Hacking the Subject: Black Feminism and Refusal beyond the
Limits of Critique" sets as its task a reconfiguration of Chandler's
reconfigurative project. Da Silva is animated by a confusion with
Chandler, or a wanting more from him, inasmuch as it is un-
clear how his desedimentation disassembles the patriarchal form
Chandler reads in Du Bois's discussion of his genealogy, a form
da Silva reads as the formal condition that permits a juridical
political subject to be enunciated. Desedimentation, da Silva
argues, operates within the patriarchal form—with which I agree,
hence the necessity to think gender problematics explicitly—so
it is necessary, in her language, to hack the figure of the X.

Her aim ultimately is to articulate the utility of "the female
figure of blackness" staging a confrontation, or intervention, a
more radical desedimentation, in relation to the notion of the
subject, the object, and the other.[5] This confrontation comes
from a lineage of "unacceptable women" like Sojourner Truth,
whom da Silva marks as a spectral interlocutor, and explicitly
genders the "Negro" as the gesture for problematizing the problematic thought. Using Chandler's book and his discourse on

5. da Silva, 21.

Du Bois as a critical point of departure, da Silva homes in on the question of the paternal and patriarchal in a way that opens up a gendered space. She subsequently deploys Spillers's female flesh ungendered as what she deems a hack of the Chandlerian X in order to reconfigure Du Bois's unnamed great-grandmother—the subject in Du Bois's text, on Chandler's reading, who cannot be named and thus bears only the "name" of the X—as an antipatriarchal analytic.

I want to utilize da Silva's theorizing as an evidentiary tangent, or supportive thrust, to prove my understanding of the X's double duty as both racial (black; Negro) and gender (trans; gender nonnormative) problem. A hacked system causes a problem, so hacking the X, which itself is already a hacking of a system, entails the problematizing of a problem. Blackness's problem for thought is compounded by transness's problem for gender. Both's situatedness in the figure of the X gives the letter, as figurative, over to a significatory problematizing that rummages around in the dregs of ontology in order to interrogate, to problematize, the project of purity—whether racial origins, locatable gendered corporeality, or both. To hack this overarching project allows me to argue for the inextricability of blackness and transness by way of their referentiality, by which it is meant that the black and the gender nonnormative overlap in order to demonstrate byzantine nodes of the critique of what Sylvia Wynter calls Man.[6] I am thus figuring both, by way of Chandler, in the figure of the X, theorizing the X's utility in highlighting all of this.

The hacked X ($\backslash$X) must refuse determination and acts as a referent for (the figure of) indeterminacy. This indeterminacy connotes gender nonnormativity's hegemonic indeterminacy, and trans and transed gender make their mark on refusing external

6. See Snorton, *Black on Both Sides*.

determination from without. With this, however, is an abiding blackness, and the indeterminacy that connotes transness also, simultaneously, is proposed by da Silva "as blackness's greatest gift."[7] Refusal of determination from rubrics fundamentally predicated on determining the totality of being proves deeply troublesome, and residing in this trouble is what the X, or the \X, continues to do on the valence of race and gender problematics. Characteristic of this indeterminacy is an undelimitable origin. Chandler puts "the African American subject" at the center of this indeterminacy, as it "is quite often 'both/and,' as well as 'neither/nor,'" emblematizing the inability to determine *or* undetermine—a radical (non)positionality of disallowing determination from anywhere (37). But the African American subject, to the extent that it is an inflection of blackness, also promotes a gender trouble by its refusal of determination. Gender self-determination is axiomatic in trans theorizing, but the "self" of this determination is one that has ecstatically unbounded itself from normative logics of self insofar as those logics necessitate inhabitation of the gender binary. It then becomes determination via a self that is not a self, a mobile subjectivity dis/located elsewhere: its subjectivity resides in the both/and *and* the neither/nor. This is the *gender* problem in the folds of Chandler's theorizations.

This is a project that yearns for a radical otherwise and outside. Looking at ourselves "in a radically *other* way" *is* the figure of the X (111), so it is perhaps the Negro and the trans that might shuttle us toward this outsidedness, or a subjectivity as outside. To be and do blackness and to be and do transness mean that we look at ourselves and others radically differently; we are and do radical difference and differentiation. This radical differ-

---

7. da Silva, "Hacking the Subject," 39n7.

ence and differentiation demands the reception of a gift. This reception is impossible, we know from Derrida, for we cannot even acknowledge the givenness of the gift without annulling it, cannot thank the giver without inducting the gift and act of giving into the economy of exchange. But the gift persists, here, in the problematics of the Negro and the trans as modalities of desedimentation that might quite literally free us from ourselves or cultivate the possibility for non-ontological being—indeed, da Silva's "being-in-the-world anew."[8] This gift *forms nothing,* da Silva says, a radical departure from theorizations of different ways to be, more or less, the same subject. For her hacked X, a gendered theorization of the X, to form nothing is to seriously claim that we are not looking to "center black women" or simply posit black people or black women as the *ground* for theorizing done on the same logics, for these are still ensnared in the logics of opposition, or ontology, or some kind of purity, whether that purity is a pristine whiteness or brooding categorical blackness. To form nothing is to take seriously that having no form, abandoning the ontological ground, *is* the desedimentation of the ontological ground. And *that* is whence we must begin anew.

Da Silva, in short, "violate[s] his [Chandler's] reading by hijacking his 'certain X' toward the ends of a radical (black feminist) praxis," which is, further, toward the end of the displacement

---

8. da Silva, 38. She says further to this point that the gift of the X, which is blackness and, too, the disruption of the gender-sexual form I am calling transness, offers a "becoming of/in the world without the presumed necessity for resolution and determination and thus without the modes of knowing—framed as the logic of opposition (Aristotle and Aquinas) or sublation (Hegel)—which always already describes existence as a scene of violence, and imposes the necessity of domination or obliteration, as in a hierarchical ordering (Natural History) or a deadly struggle for existence (Evolution), respectively."

of identity, toward an impurity that displaces pure being.[9] We get, truly, to a desedimentation of pure being when we engage the explicitly gendered, a gendered engagement that does not end at the gender question, which Spillers reprimands many, including black women, for doing; this engagement is in fact the only way to arrive at, or get closer to, the displacement of identificatory logics that are themselves, even when those identities are ones we love—black, transgender, woman, African American, and so on—to be ultimately abandoned. And another way to put this is in the language of the trans; that is, I had an anonymous reviewer on an excerpted earlier draft of these meditations insist, understandably, but overlooking the fundamental thrust of the identificatory displacement, that I talk about "actual" black transgender people. The reviewer demanded that I discuss, at length, "the concrete everyday realities of black transgender people." I get it, truly, though my body of work has been a sustained meditation—and will likely continue to be a sustained meditation for some time—on why I wish to skirt this imperative. The figuration of the Negro-cum-blackness and the trans is not reducible to people who are called black and/or transgender. I refuse the insistence on discussing, again at length, the concrete "lived experiences" of people who rest at the nexus of black and transgender (though this is not to say that those materialities and epistemologies do not inform my theorization, nor is it to say that I never discuss these things). My refusal stems from a desire for subjectivity to emerge outside of and away from the dictates inscribed in ontology. If blackness and transness displace ontological ground, we in fact *cannot* simply outline the materialities of black and transgender subjects, for to do such would not get us outside of the very logics that circumscribe such

9. da Silva, 23.

violated life, not to mention that some "black" and "trans" people *do not do black and trans work* and some who are not "black" or "trans" in fact do. As da Silva puts it, "when a subject emerges in the determination of (decision on) a gender-sexual position"—or ending at the gender question, simply accepting the transparent and untroubled validity of there being black transgender people, black cis women, and so on—"s/he hopelessly restates the positions of 'subject' and of the 'other.'" What she suggests here is that the anonymous review to which I was compelled to adhere was an attempt to disregard the radical work of moving toward a radically other logic; I was required to recapitulate the same logic, unable to displace it. But to concede the emergence of, say, black transgender people on the terms that orchestrated such a subject restates the ontological ground. For a cis man to occupy the position of valid subject is not the totality, or even primary concern, of the issue. It is, rather, "that the gender-sexual feature—referent of the patriarchal-form—requests both positions (a subject and an object)"—or the ontological ground of racial distinction and the gender binary require a subject (white, cis, male) and an object (black, trans, femme) in order for subjectivities to be legibly organized.[10]

I offer, then, a series of imaginative—or aspirative, unknown and unknowable, outside the bounds of even the imagination—claims Chandler provides for a new civilization.

> I am proposing . . . a generosity without limit—as the opening toward another form of "civilization" altogether.
>   That is to say,
>
>> – beyond all problems of *remembrance* (although an unfungible, necessary reference);
>> – beyond all existing *forms of limit* (which must yet be

10. da Silva, 25.

ceaselessly engaged, challenged, displaced, and disman-
tled); and even,
- beyond what we can yet inhabit as *imagination* (which
must still be affirmed without reservation, even in the
form of desire [the twinkle in the eye]);
- the "African Diaspora" or, better, the general problem
of the Negro as a problem for thought may be taken as a
theoretical name for the possibility (and necessity) that
a new organization or constellation of historicity (across
the centuries to come) will have been inaugurated in the
ceaselessly redoubled, disseminated, practices by which
a certain (mobile and strictly undelimitable) *we* has been
constructed for itself and for others. (174–75, emphasis
original)

This new civilization is begotten, perhaps primarily or solely,
by way of understanding the X as racial and gender hack, in da
Silva's sense, as she, too, alludes to something akin to Chandler
when she yearns for what "the gift of the X" could bring, that is,
possibility, a new way of being-in-the-world unviolated, undeter-
mined, or being-out-the-world-in-the-world. A new civilization
goes by alternative ethics and relations, different and differing
logics. If the oppositional logic of the current system is inadequate, its binary logic too stultifying and necessarily disrupted
by the Negro and gender problem, what we must imagine toward
is another sort of logic, an (il)logic perhaps, or what Chandler
gestures toward as "the radical possibility of this other logic" (4).
Syntactic skewering, grammatical upheavals, rhetorical oddities,
ontological impossibilities, and the like must characterize our
new way of being in our new civilization, if *civilization* is even an
apt term for such an environ. Our constellations will morph and
shift into things we could never have anticipated. We will live,
hopefully, simply in the beyond, in a place that is placeless, a horizon unattainable yet attained in our pursuit of its impossibility.

Hack the X, irrupting the chromosomal and the sexed binary
that makes use of it, problematizing the order of purity where

"order" and "purity" buttress the taxonomic categorization in which violence inheres. For X to be hacked is not to disrupt *it*; for X to be hacked is, in no uncertain terms, to proliferate the proliferative, which destroys polarities that organize a Manichean world. Hacking the X is precisely the aim of *The Problem of the Negro as a Problem for Gender*: if X serves as a hack to an order of totalizing purity marked and inaugurated by whiteness, the hacked X, which might be to say the transing of X, the trans of the X, is to problematize the problematic of blackness—to demonstrate how the problematic of blackness is, too, endemically, a problematic of and for gender. Chandler overlooks one of the subject's forms (the patriarchal) while undermining, generatively, another (the racial). He gains footing to undermine and desediment the racial distinction by leaving sedimented the gender distinction, or the gender binary. To desediment racial and gender distinction, to hack the X that is already a reconfigurative figure, is more than a deconstructive move toward another possible determination (recall Lamonda Horton-Stallings's critique of an "(un)naming" which seeks to unname in order to later rename in favor of "unnaming" or leaving indeterminate); it is a desedimentary move, a hack, a figuration of indeterminacy.

This is to gesture toward the polysemous anoriginally displaced site that is the Negro and gender problem. Put differently, origins are never original and pure; all those who yearn for the purity of the before-"white"-folks-came and, as many of my incarcerated students misguidedly say, "turned brother against brother" or had "black" people "selling their own into slavery," yearn for a myth. There was no pure, unadulterated African unity. Indeed, there was no "Africa," no racialized blackness that connected all the denizens of the second largest continent; it is fallacious to believe "that very deep continuities supervene upon skin color," and those yearners possess an unyielding "conviction that if you traveled back in time and dropped the needle on a James Brown album, Cleo[patra] would instantly break out into the Camel Walk. The hope and belief that we cherish is not so much a proposition about melanin and physiognomy; it's the proposition that beneath the scales of time and through the mists of history Cleopatra was a sister."[11] So, too, are the gender binary and natal assignations of "sex"—which, it bears being stated, is not a transparent category or objective description but rather, and always, a fiction that is inaccessible outside of what has been deemed gender[12]—believed to possess an origin at which we can arrive and glean objective truth. It is presumed that there is an originary point of cohesion to discern sex or gender, located either in the genitals, the brain, the chromosomes, or what have you. But this also proves dismally fallacious, as gender as well as sex are always dis/located, bound by no agreed-upon point of discernment, and mutable (a mutability that shifts all the more radically when circulating with blackness). The gendered "origin" of, say, the technician who deems a fetus "a boy!" during a sonogram is enacting a political interpellation, drawing the fetus into boyness rather than observing an untampered-with facticity. The declaration is neither innocent nor pure.

Thus "*there is no from.* There is no there, or somewhere, or place that a black from is anchored to," as Katherine McKittrick

11. Henry Louis Gates, *Tradition and the Black Atlantic: Critical Theory in the African Diaspora* (New York: BasicCivitas, 2010), 139–40.

12. See Judith Butler, *Bodies That Matter: On the Discursive Limits of "Sex"* (New York: Routledge, 2011), xv. Specifically, Butler notes that gender seems always to absorb sex, making sex unable to be gotten to in such a way that it is radically outside of linguistic, social, and cultural productions of meaning: "If gender is the social construction of sex, and if there is no access to this 'sex' except by means of its construction," Butler writes, "then it appearsnot only that sex is absorbed by gender, but that 'sex' becomes something like a fiction, perhaps a fantasy, retroactively installed at a prelinguistic site to which there is no direct access."

argues; the origin of blackness and, too, gender is radically displaced, so much so that it is radically *nowhere*—what McKittrick goes on to notate as "the fantastic nowhere of blackness."[13] To have no origin, which constructs the black and trans as arising from nowhereness and nothingness—from Colebrook's transitivity—is to desediment any ontological mooring from either of these historicized figures. The figures, ultimately, are empty, unfigured, and hence mobilized as anoriginal ontological dislodgings. The Negro and the trans, the black and nonnormatively gendered, become not figures as such or identifiable corporeal subjects; instead, and primarily, they ping the residue of what cannot and indeed refuses to exist under extant conditions of possibility. Having no Africanic or biologically binaristic from to anchor figuration, blackness and transness subsequently have no designated "to," leaving the future open-ended, radically, and serving *as* that open-ended futurity. They hack subjectivity; they hack the future of what we might become.

The purpose of articulating the Negro and trans as problematics is to render purportedly originary and pure sites of, in this instance, race and gender as deviantly generative for otherwise ends. The X and its hacking are the indexation of an alternative possibility that exceeds how racial and gender taxonomies have been operationalized and now proves as "the recognition of the generative capacity that might arise by way of an affirmation of difference in human relation at all levels of social and historical generality," Chandler writes.[14] Affirming difference is

13. Katherine McKittrick, "Commentary: Worn Out," *Southeastern Geographer* 57, no. 1 (2017): 97, 99, emphasis original, https://doi.org/10.1353/sgo.2017.0008.

14. Nahum Dimitri Chandler, "Introduction: On the Virtues of Seeing—at Least, but Never Only—Double," *CR: The New Centennial Review* 12, no. 1 (2012): 3, https://doi.org/10.1353/ncr.2012.0034.

to hack the X, to precipitate the problematizing of a problematic. Recognition that the Negro viz. blackness arises not from a purity in history but indexes precisely the "multiple forms of genesis, always both diverse and re-inaugurating, in the instance of an originary irruption" necessitates the recognition—though perhaps more closely a nonrecognition, a hacking of the interpellative gesture—of the trans viz. nonnormative gender and gender problematic as radically *an*originally displaced, resting nowhere, bearing no "truth" in a discernible location, always dispossessed and dispersed from the jump that disallows the very move toward natality.[15]

15. Chandler, 2.

Uninscriptions

The proper names are already no longer proper names,
because their production is their obliteration, because the
erasure and the imposition of the letter are originary, because they do not supervene upon a proper inscription; it
is because the proper name has never been, as the unique
appellation reserved for the presence of a unique being,
anything but the original myth of a transparent legibility
present under the obliteration.

—JACQUES DERRIDA, *Of Grammatology*

Now, one hears from a long time ago that "white is merely
a state of mind." I add to that, white is a moral choice. It's
up to you to be as white as you want to be and pay the
price of that ticket. You cannot tell a black man by the
color of skin, either.

—JAMES BALDWIN, *"Black English: A Dishonest Argument"*

WHAT WOULD IT MEAN to possibly reject, as we seem to be called
to do in Chandler's text—not to mention da Silva and Derrida,
Moten and Spillers, among others—the grounds that provide our
legibility? No, dead ass: what would it mean to reject, *as an ethical imperative,* ontological grounds of legibility, rooted in purity
and demarcation, which is to say to reject the things given to us
as our existence even though, I would submit, those things are
violences—racial identities predicated on racial distinction and

taxonomies, gender identities predicated on gender distinction and the gender binary? What would it mean not to recapitulate the very logics we are seeking to undermine even if the refusal of recapitulation makes us uncomfortable?

The briefest but perhaps most biting chapter of Chandler's text is "The Souls of an Ex-White Man," in which he reads Du Bois's meditation on John Brown:

> Du Bois describes a melancholic John Brown, compelled to challenge the very terms of his fate or death. In doing so, the narrative that his life and precipitate death makes possible outlines a tear in the fabric of providence, and thus marks his struggle with the limits that have been bestowed upon him as privilege. It moves in some tenacious relationship of maintenance or affirmation, as well as a sense of loss, of the sense of possible being that has been withdrawn, the ways of being a "white" man that have been marked as beyond the acceptable or the normal, that is, the ways of being other than a "White" man. (114–15)

John Brown died twice, Chandler argues. Indeed, Brown was executed on December 2, 1859, for treason, murder, and insurrection. This is the death on the historical record. This was the death of the flesh-and-blood man. But he died another time, or rather something Brown was, not born but, coerced to be in order to exist in the world as such died, or was killed by the subject who was executed. This other death was to create a life, an unsanctioned life. The person we call John Brown understood that he was "a 'White' man," a social designation he did not want and, I would assert, jettisoned. He understood "that in order for him to live he must give this socially granted life over to death (or not to live, or to maintain himself only within a kind of death by living as a 'White' man); or rather, we might say, that in order to live, he had to take this socially and historically granted life and dispense with it, kill it, destroy it, give it up to the risk and possibility of absolute dissolution" (115). This death is what intrigues me; this death demonstrates that not only is the figure of the Negro a historicized figure made to exist within a certain corporeal delimitation but the problematics that inhere in the figuration of, as it were, Negroness, a Negroness that is an imperfect nominative (as all nominatives are) for the desedimentation of pure being, are truly an open desedimentary terrain that even "white" people have the capacity to take on. Brown is recognized as possessive of a "fundamental and radical orientation" toward Negro figuratives, or the desedimentation of pure being unfixed from a historicized subject, making due on the generalization Chandler proffers as that which is to be mobilized around. John Brown became problematic; John Brown became *a paraontological Negro*. Blackness, in its paraontology and the taking seriously of that paraontology, can and must be mobilized by any and all who commit to radicality and ontological desedimentation named in that insurrectionary radicality. So yes, John Brown might have been a hell of a lot blacker than even Darnell next door.[1]

1. A little cheeky, a little contentious, I know. But I need to say it, as I've said it in multiple places before. I'm drawing here largely, in addition to Chandler, on Moten and the elucidating work of George Shulman. It might be easiest for me simply to quote Shulman: "As the name for life's animating and undoing excess, blackness provokes forms of order. . . . Blackness thus connotes aspects of life that anyone can—and all need to—acknowledge (UC, 50). Moten thereby conceives the life made by those marked black in terms neither ethnically closed nor symbolically foreclosed, but politically and aesthetically open." Shulman continues in a footnote, "Indeed, blackness is 'before the binary said to define our existence' and 'older than Africa' (SL, 21). For him, 'blackness is a general force of fugitivity that racialization in general, and the more specific instantiation of the color line, exacerbate and focus without originating' (UM, 35). He thus denies 'that blackness is a property that belongs to blacks' (BN, 750)." See George Shulman, "Fred Moten's Refusals and Consents: The Politics of Fugitivity," *Political Theory* (2020): 12, 36n21.

My concern is twofold. First, like Chandler, I do not intend to say that Brown *was* a Negro, that historically identifiable dark-skinned subject. Brown neither "became *a* Negro" nor did he "arrive" at, once and for all, a status of not-white (or not-White). The point being made is that he produced a kind of subjectivity for himself via "the strange movement of a 'White' man becoming 'otherwise,' other than simply 'white,' perhaps" (117). I am unsure if there is a name for this kind of subject, which would amount to a nonsubject inasmuch as he is, to whatever extent, relinquished from the ontological grounds governing existence: the ground of being within the dictates of racial distinction and governing others and oneself by their constitutive requisites.

Second, I wish to understand the gesture of "ex-ness," the gesture of being and becoming an "ex-white man," as consequential on both registers of the identificatory descriptor. That is, Brown was indeed one who rebuked whiteness and thus was an ex-white. But what is left that might be revealed when thinking through the valences of what it could mean, what it could do, to be an ex-white *man,* or more generally an ex-*man*? Or, I might cheekily articulate this as, how might we become *X-men,* galvanizing the discussion of the X again for the purposes of marking it as a gendered uninscription?[2] These are my concerns for this final chapter.

The person we call John Brown knew it was demanded that he be a "'White' man." But he in effect renounced whiteness, becoming, with a necessary linguistic precision, in proximity to and emerging through the miasmic sociosubjective ether that

2. This echoes resoundingly with nonbinary writer Joshua M. Ferguson, who writes, "The X-Men were one of my favourite super-hero teams growing up, and the treatment of their mutations bears a striking analogy to the experience of LGBTQ people. And now, I am literally an 'X-(Man)/(male).'" See Ferguson, *Me, Myself, They,* 207.

mobilizes blackness. It is held that "the ultimate premise of racial distinction," or the foundation of racialization and racializing taxonomies necessary for social legibility, is "a categorical or oppositional logic of distinction or identification" (121). White supremacy and the racial identities it fashioned gain traction via the validation of categorical distinctions that take the names of races we are called and call ourselves. These categorical imperatives—which is part of white supremacist taxonomizing logics, that in order to be understood as a valid subject, we must inhabit one of the existential options it has fashioned—cannot hold if we are to eradicate white supremacy's ills. You know, race is the child, not the parent or guardian, of racism and all that.[3] Brown, then, in unbecoming white, as it were, did so via a *transing* of the categorical imperative. And I might say, too, without undermining the possibility of enacting behaviors implied to gender privileges, in unbecoming white, and insofar as he was forced to be a certain iteration of whiteness via his induction into being and doing himself as *white man,* Brown also transed the "man" of his white man-ness. That is, as a required "'White' man," the "man" was constitutive of his whiteness, thus to unbecome, to rebuke, to trans the white is to also, necessarily, trans the man.

Brown arises through, Chandler says, the *meaning* of the Negro. He emerges onto the social scene askew, or whatever might be said of the representationality, the "look," of one who emerged precisely through how he vitiated the conditions of his natal and prescribed (and proscribed) emergence. To say that Brown comes to us as a figure by way of asserting himself, promiscuously, illegally even, through the meaning and implication and generalizable desedimentary theoretical praxis of the Negro

3. See, e.g., Ta-Nehisi Coates, *Between the World and Me* (New York: Spiegel and Grau, 2015), 7. Coates writes, unfortunately with patrilineal language, "But race is the child of racism, not the father."

is to present "the Negro," in Chandler's terms, as a figured figure, or as, again in Chandler's terms, a material *idea*, a problematic, an exorbitance. Brown did not become black, a Negro, but perhaps he became toward a certain kind of Negroness inasmuch as the figure of the Negro, an iterative Negroness, references a desedimentary X that we've established to be an interminable racial and gender indeterminacy. This is to say that Brown stands "within the historical consciousness of the Negro in America" (127) and on these grounds—impure nongrounds—shares an affinity with that which we refer to as paraontology, desedimentation, problematizing, impure nonbeing: the Negro, the trans.

To make the argument that John Brown is not only an ex-white but also, consequentially, an ex-white *man* is a tricky one. If Chandler argues that Du Bois understands Brown as "melancholic," we must heed "*gender* as a kind of *melancholy*."[4] Brown's melancholy also pervaded his gendered assignation. I am not proffering the claim that Brown made intentional assertions of his "being" a woman or genderqueer or nonbinary; he, to my mind, made no such claims. What he did do, though, is vitiate the tenets upon which whiteness rests, rendering him, effectively, an ex-white. And the tenets upon which whiteness rests include normative gender, cisgender masculinity in Brown's case; thus to dissolve the tethers stitching together a coherent whiteness is also a dissolution of his normative masculinity. He X'ed his "manness," refusing all perinatal and sociohistorical requirements to remain an essential, which is to say pure, being.

The whole theoretical enterprise of desedimentation is an evacuation of essence, and evacuating essentialism of its teeth has long been a black and trans, and black feminist, project. In other words, following philosopher Catherine Malabou—with

4. Judith Butler, "Melancholy Gender—Refused Identification," *Psychoanalytic Dialogues* 5, no. 2 (1995): 166, emphasis added.

whom my twenty-year-old self fell in intellectual love during a yearlong philosophy seminar—to the extent that desedimentation is linked to deconstruction, it is imperative that we also understand the undertaking as "deconstructing the idea of biological rigidity and showing, once again, that there are no grounds for a concept of essence, conceived of as substance, be it ontological or natural. Transformability is at work from the start, it trumps all determination."[5] To engage desedimentation, a refined kind of deconstruction, is to eschew the belief in biological rigidity as manifesting itself in any kind of substance (or materiality). This is to trump all determination, all essentialist predication. Racial and gender distinctions are determinations, essentialisms, rigidities. John Brown enacts a desedimentation and is thus deconstructing biological rigidities, among which racial *and* gender distinctions are chief. Brown's ex-ness is that of an ex-*white man*. Brown's protestation, his ex-ness (and indeed his X-ness), is a working of himself away from the scene(s) of legibility, which are the scenes of a demanded white manness. In working away from these—both of these—he effectively disembodies himself. (And some wonder why "the body" does not show up much in my work: it is the scene, as it were, of the ontological crime.) In disembodying himself, he falls away from, or more agentially moves away from, the premises on which bodyness rests, backed by an ontological ground. Rejection of the ontological ground leaves one unembodied, in a sense, which is also to be catapulted away from the very identificatory registers that latch onto footholds that go by the names, among others, of race and gender. It leaves one uninscribed.

My purpose here, then, is to mark Brown, not to the exclusion

5. Catherine Malabou, *Changing Difference* (Malden, Mass.: Polity, 2011), 139.

of a vast array of others,[6] as a subjective example of uninscription. We are inscribed onto the sociohistorical ledger in order to exist as such under the heading of the ontological project that curtails how and even that we exist in any particular way. The inscription, the Heideggarian thrownness, is orchestrated by what is permitted as a valid emergent onto the scene, which acts as a legibilization. To be uninscribed is the paraontological project, the project of the X (crossing out), the project of desedimentation. Uninscription bears a markedly gendered valence that converges with Chandler's racial theorization in a way generative for the ultimate articulation of the Negro's problematics as mobilized by, precipitative of, and coeval with gender prob-

6. I want to be very clear in this subclause, as there is the strong possibility that some might use the pedestaling of a white person as the figure through which I make the claim of exemplarity as evidence of the privileges of whiteness. That I am homing in on John Brown to assert the paraontological movement away from racial and gender distinction, that the privileges of whiteness even allow a white subject to "be" a Negro, will be read, by some, as blasphemy. This, to me, is to overlook the seriousness and abolitionist radicality of the fundamental argument that Chandler, and my reading of him, is making, namely, that (1) "the Negro" is not first and foremost a historical figure and thus is not confined to certain epidermally delimited subjects; (2) the rejection of whiteness—the serious, thoroughgoing rejection, wherein one risks oneself ontologically and existentially, as Brown did—is not to be subsumed into white privilege but a radical movement toward the demands of blackness; and (3) it is not the aim to hedge the claim of the Negro as a figurative figure who, if solely a historical figure, perpetuates the logics of ontology and pure being, and the claim of racial distinction as the product of whiteness and white supremacy, undergirded by the ontological project. Taking these claims seriously necessitates that one look for where the desedimentary work is happening, and some of those locations are in figures one would deem "white" and "men." This does not exclude or subordinate people who are identified as black and women and trans, for example, but it also must not require them as the sole exemplars, the only valid evidentiary citations.

lematics. "It's taken a lot of resistance," T Fleischmann begins their musings on being uninscribed,

> that I want to leave my gender and my sex life uninscribed—that it took me years to consider the fact that I did not have to name my gender or sexuality at all, so that now I must always tell people that I am not something. I insist on this absence more, even, than I used to insist on my identities. . . . The uninscribed, like Gonzalez-Torres says, is a site of change, where I might understand my actual context and do something about it, rather than getting tangled up in a game of words, and so that is where I would like to focus. I am of course still written into this whole structure, I can't escape the language, but that won't stop me from refusing it anyway, and believing that a blank paper might transport me somewhere else.[7]

In being uninscribed, one gives oneself over to movement. It is a refusal to name oneself because one knows that the name will ultimately be inadequate, it coming from the language available, a language from without and dictatorial of how we can exist. This language, we know, cannot be escaped entirely, but we refuse it anyway, knowing there is the possibility of being blank, blanked, uninscribed onto the page, our presence not a matter of how we are written but perhaps of the shadows that accrue briefly when the page is creased and crumpled. Uninscriptions unmark sites of change, of movement, of absence that vex the requisites of the scene. If we must be inscribed, we demand to be inscribed un-ly, crossed and X'ed out, annotated, redacted, misspelled, and run-on.

The mellifluously cacophonous concatenation between the Negro and the trans, or what could be said to fall under a heading iterated as Negro problematics and gender problematics, finds a certain figuration in the terminology of uninscription. For one

7. T Fleischmann, *Time Is the Thing a Body Moves Through* (Minneapolis, Minn.: Coffee House Press, 2019), 64.

to uninscribe oneself from, say, racial distinction entails something that looks like what John Brown did. Such an uninscription means that one *dies*. One dies as the subject one was given over as in order to become another subject or, since to die as, say, "White" when one is told one must be a "'White' man" desediments the ontological ground gifting one with subjectivity, to become no subject. Brown was an ontological insurrection. They didn't know what to do with him because he was monstrous: a "'White' man" who did not want to be, and indeed *was not,* after a self-murder, white. Such a subject is unfathomable and thus must be eradicated in order to maintain ontological ground. Put another way, all those who go about life being white men because they are told they are white men, believe they are white men, want there to be other white men, are pure beings. And that is to say, they were beings. John Brown, however, was an impure being, a white man who was not, and did not want to be, white. Purity is constitutive of being, so Brown's impurity negated his being. And because of this, *he* was negated.

The paradoxical impure being John Brown became was the subject on the other side, the underside, of the Negro problematic. John Brown uninscribed himself without making recourse to the displeasure of widely held descriptions of deconstruction, to reinscription. He moved with the Negro, desedimented, on no ground—"disintegrate[d] . . . ground."[8]

We thus demand the obliteration of the ground enabling ontology, which means we obliterate the subject as we know it. The radical project of Negro and gender problematics demands it; if the problem of the Negro is indeed a problem for gender, the two swirling toward a fundamentally desedimentary project,

8. Stefano Harney and Fred Moten, *The Undercommons: Fugitive Planning and Black Study* (Wivenhoe, U.K.: Minor Compositions, 2013), 132.

ontological grounds cannot hold. Hence, the subject, that by-product of ontological grounds, cannot hold. We will require something else entirely. John Brown was an ex-white man. I own that assertion along with Chandler and Du Bois. John Brown was also, unowned by Chandler or Du Bois, an ex-man, which is to say that both normative masculinity and maleness are constitutive of whiteness, a loosening of the latter necessitating a loosening, a transing, of the former; and additionally, to unmoor the purity of ontological grounds is also and always to unfix ontological ground's attending constituents, chief among them not only "race" but "gender" as well. I am saying neither that Brown was a Negro nor that he was transgender/woman. I *am* saying that he was neither white nor man—he indexes a subjective mobilization through the problematic figuration that inheres in the movement of the Negro and the trans. He was an ex–*white man,* double emphasis; he was an *X*-white man.

Acknowledgments

I decided to write this because I was frustrated. And, too, because I was seduced. Chandler's text pissed me off with its esoteric writing—the kind of writing I actually tend to love—and it also, because of this, seduced me into grappling with it intensely, with its wondrousness and its omissions. His writing invited me to engage it and to critique it on its own behalf. So, I thank you, Nahum, if I may.

Too, I must thank Jason Weidmann, who supported the submission of this manuscript from the very beginning, and Leah Pennywark, who graciously and kindly talked me through its conceptual ideas and gifted me with crucial sources to strengthen my argument. And how could I not thank those who exercised these ideas with me and shared in my frustration: Jesse and Terrell and Biko, who all, in different ways, cowrote my thoughts alongside me; and, by discursive proxy, Denise Ferreira da Silva, whose work is, always, indispensable.

And to all those students (namely, Jack, with those three-plus-hour Zoom chats) and colleagues and audience members who listened to me ramble, spewing everything from nonsense to gold: you are in this, too, and you have mattered, at the very least, profoundly, to me.

(Continued from page iii)

Forerunners: Ideas First

Marquis Bey is assistant professor of African American studies and English, and core member of the critical theory cluster, at Northwestern University.